Afterlife for the Living

Make Every Moment Matter

Dr. Bernice N. King-Strong

authorHOUSE®

AuthorHouse™
1663 Liberty Drive
Bloomington, IN 47403
www.authorhouse.com
Phone: 833-262-8899

Published by AuthorHouse   07/07/2023

ISBN: 979-8-8230-1120-4 (sc)
ISBN: 979-8-8230-1121-1 (e)

Library of Congress Control Number: 2023912060

Print information available on the last page.

*Any people depicted in stock imagery provided by Getty Images are models,
and such images are being used for illustrative purposes only.
Certain stock imagery © Getty Images.*

This book is printed on acid-free paper.

For

My Entire Family

Edney
Green
James
King
Lewis
Lorthridge
Strong
Walker

Epigraph

Afterlife for the Living: Make Every Moment Matter

Afterlife refers to the past life of the deceased. The idea for the book, *Afterlife for the Living,* was born after the sudden death of our son, and out of a desire to help those survivors after the loss of a loved one to understand how we can survive and should honor their lives. It is vital that each bereaved and grieving individual find their own way of maneuvering and narrating the path ahead to deal with what life presents as we start this new journey.

The two terms bereavement and grief, although similar in nature, have different meanings. Bereavement refers specifically to the process of regaining your emotional, mental, and physical equilibrium from the death of a loved one. Meanwhile, grief is a reaction to any form of loss. Both bereavement and grief include a wide range of feelings from deep sadness to anger. Adapting to the loss does vary from one person to the next. According to Good therapy (2017), "The reaction to loss is colored by a person's background, beliefs, relationship to what was lost, and other factors". Regardless of the circumstances of the loss know this to be true:

On beginning to live in the afterlife of a loved one, a poem:

It is okay to be afraid of things you do not understand.
It is okay to feel anxious when things are not working your way.
It is okay to feel lonely... even when you are with other people.
It is okay to feel unfulfilled because you know something is missing.
It is okay to think, worry and cry.
It is okay to do whatever you have to do, but just remember, too...
Eventually you are going to adjust to the changes that life brings your way.

And you will realize that it is okay to love again and laugh again.
And it is okay to get to the point where the life you live.
Is full and satisfying and good to you…
And it will be that way because you made it that way.

-Anonymous

Acknowledgements

My deepest appreciation to colleagues, family and friends for contributing to this book. Thanks to Adrienne Bernice Strong and Carmen Strong Echols for contributing to this effort and for their encouragement to finish a project long overdue. Thanks to the following people for sharing their stories of loss and their contributions to Chapters on Child Loss, Grandparent Loss, Sibling Loss, Spousal Loss and Suicide. The list of contributors who offered their heartfelt inspiration to help us all grow and thrive in our afterlives:

Adrienne Bernice Strong
Carmen Bernice Strong Echols
Eleanor
Kristen Duncan Gillespie
Sam
Sharon Walton Shead
Shirley Baker Shields
Tommy Klop
Victoria
Anonymous

Revelation 21:4: (KJV)

"He will wipe every tear from their eyes. There will be no more death or mourning or crying or pain, for the old order of things has passed away."

Introduction

Everyone will experience bereavement, grief, and loss, and will live through it differently. We experience many emotions when we go through the grieving process. Understanding the process of grief and the many facets of it helps us to identify where we are on the continuum of the grieving process. Since the beginning of time, we have grieved losses. Although the emotions we felt were not categorized, we had the emotions just the same. We experienced ebbs and flows throughout this process. Despite the universality of grief emotion, every individual goes through the phases of grief at their own unique pace, even though there are commonalities that are evident when we are in one stage as opposed to another. It is important to note that the grieving process is not linear. We may revisit stages that we have gone through previously. There is no set timetable for grief; anyone who tells you to "move on" or "get over it" is underestimating and misunderstanding the weight of loss. The length of your grieving process depends on what kind of grief you are experiencing. Understanding the various stages of mourning and grief helps us to recognize how we are continuing through our grief journey. Therefore, we are more able to categorize where we are and develop strategies to better cope as we experience each stage.

It was not until 1969 that we were able to categorize the feelings that we emoted when experiencing grief and bereavement. Elizabeth Kubler Ross (1969) was the first to categorize the feelings expressed during grief in her book titled, On *Death and Dying (1969)*. She identified the five stages of grief after a loss and these stages are summarized below:

Denial- Denial refers to the difficulty comprehending the reality of a loss. Although there are ways in which denial is manifested, here are some examples (not all inclusive) of the symptoms of this stage. Symptoms of denial during the grieving process might include (1) Believing that there has been a mistake and your loved one is not gone. (2) continuing to speak about your deceased loved one in the present tense.

Anger- Anger is a perfectly natural response, and in the case of loss, it can be directed at a collection of sources. It can also manifest as blame- the feeling that someone is at fault for loss. You might feel angry with yourself for some perceived role in the loss, or even at your loved one for dying. You are angry at doctors or first responders for "letting" your loved one die, or at God for letting something so unfair and tragic happen.

As with every stage of grief, these emotions can be experienced in reaction to non-death losses, too. You may have lost your employment and feel angry at the colleague who took on your job responsibilities. Or you lost your home because you could no longer afford the mortgage payments, leaving you angry at the state of the economy. Your anger could also be less targeted, less sensible; not always rational.

Bargaining- The bargaining process sometimes happens during the period of anticipated loss. In the instance of a terminal illness, we bargain that if we recover, we promise to do better in life. Bargaining also takes place after a loss. An example would be, "if only" thinking:

Each of us will manage our grief in a manner like the way we manage everyday life. The goal to keep in mind is to emerge from our pain and loss and make something positive be the result of our experience. Whether the loss was that of a child, parent, grandparent, sibling, close friend, or pet. All loss is felt, but the intensity of the loss corresponds to the relationship you had with the deceased and sometimes the circumstances of their death. Some examples are (1) "If only we had gone to a different doctor, maybe she could have been treated in time". (2) "If only I had put my dog on a leash, she would not have run into the oncoming traffic."

Depression -It is normal to experience sorrow when someone you love dies or when you have experienced another major loss. Symptoms of the depression stage of grief can include: (1) Loss of hope for the future. (2) Feeling directionless, lost, or confused about your life. (3) Difficulty concentrating and impaired ability to make decisions.

Grief-related depression often results in physical symptoms, too, like aches and pains and changes in sleep patterns. Studies show that it can even cause increased inflammation in your body, which can worsen existing health issues and lead to new ones. The depression stage of grieving is different from major depressive disorder, also known as major depression or clinical depression, a mental health condition that combines a number of emotional, cognitive, and physical symptoms. It is important to address your grief and seek help to avoid it from becoming clinical depression.

Acceptance- The mourning and sense of loss of grief may never fully fade. The acceptance stage represents learning to live with the loss-a newfound ability to acknowledge the reality of your loss and to allow sorrow and joy to live alongside one another. In this stage of grief, you are no longer paralyzed by your sadness. "Acceptance is a sense of understanding that there is a finality to what has happened."

Each of us will manage our grief in a manner similar to the way we manage everyday life. The goal in mind is to emerge from our pain and loss and make something positive be the result of our experience...whether the loss was that of a child, parent, grandparent, sibling, close friend, or pet. All loss is felt, but the intensity of the loss corresponds to the relationship we had with the deceased, and sometimes the circumstances of their death.

The information contained in this book will be familiar to some and unfamiliar information for most. After the loss of a loved one, there are multifaceted responses from survivors. How to handle one of the most stressful events in our lives needs to be fraught with coping responses that help us to deal with the hurting that succeeds a loss. Although the topics of bereavement and grief are the main themes of the book, each chapter can be read in isolation from the others. As we live and breathe, we will suffer multiple losses over a lifetime.

The chapters of this book have been arranged to assist you when dealing with losses that are similar in nature. The following overview will assist you in locating the topic that you are seeking. Know this scripture to be true:

All go unto one place.
All are of the dust,
And all turn to dust again. Ecclesiastes 3: 20 (KJV)

Overview

To assist readers to locate particular topics of interest in this book, please find the following outline of sections and their respective topics.

Part 1: Chapters 1-5:
These chapters discuss the occasion of bringing life into the world and having to take part in planning for celebration of life and witness the burial of that same life. Ruminations about the loss of a child; spouse, and parent.

Part 2: Chapters 6-10:
Chapters in this part explore grandparent loss and sibling loss, and how an individual may be affected during the life cycle. Miscarriage, stillbirth, sudden infant death and Infant mortality due to maternal opioid addiction are areas touched upon.

Part 3: Chapters 11-15
Topics explored in these five chapters concentrate on accidental death, violent death, murder, suicide/assisted suicide and euthanasia.

Part 4: Chapters 16-20:
This section's chapters center on friend loss, pet loss, how men and women grieve differently, the grief of special populations, and cultural responses to loss.

Part 5: Chapters 21 and 22
To sum it all up, these chapters speak to how we reinvent ourselves and live life after we have encountered the life altering experience of losing a loved one.

Moments for reflection:

Who was the most recent loss of a loved one that you have suffered? Before reading this text, think about where you are in your emotional rumination. Write about it.

Prologue

We had taken a full course of the Lamaze classes and read the Doctor Spock book. We felt that we knew everything to do when the time came. My bags had been packed for days; our son was not due until the middle of December, but he had his own timetable. He was five weeks premature; so, the doctor's said. We arrived at the hospital in the wee hours of the morning and Doc, my spouse, was able to stay with me during the entire process. I was progressing so slowly. It was 10:00 a.m. in the morning and we had been there since 3:00 a.m. I was getting nowhere. At about noon time, I was hungry and thirsty. I was only allowed to have ice chips for my dry mouth. I could not get up and walk around, but I could turn on my side. Things started to progress a bit and the contractions were stronger and closer, but very bearable. The doctor felt that I was not dilating enough. When the clock showed 1:00 p.m. it was then decided that they would give me visceral and pitocin; try that on an empty stomach! The visceral made me vomit continuously leaving me wiped out. I was so tired by then and the contractions were strong and close. Needless to say, I was upset and in severe distress. I did not want to go through with a natural delivery and asked if I could go home. I was delirious with pain. I wanted this to be over. I was wheeled into the delivery room. Two nurses started to push on the top of my abdomen and told me to push. Doc held my shoulders and back in an upward posture. I wondered if I would live through this ordeal. Suddenly, the doctor said, "another good push," and he was right. A little baby boy. He said "push again" I wondered why. I got what we came here for. I thought I had suffered enough.

The nurse places Brandon on my chest. He is so warm and small. We both looked to see who he looked like. I was wheeled out of delivery briefly. I supposed this was the usual mode of operation, what did I know, this was my first rodeo. Two friends who were present in the waiting room said he looked like me. I thought he looked like his father. I sat up. I am feeling fine now. I was instructed to lie down. The baby is taken away. I am wheeled to recovery. I am catharized because my abdomen is distended, and I was unable to void.

By now, I am more exhausted and sleepier than before. I typically slept on my stomach. I turned over and experienced the joy of being able to lie flat again. It was a while before the baby was brought back to me. When I awoke, the nurse brought the baby in. He looked different now that he was cleaned. His eyes are closed, and he is visibly very sleepy. I am supposed to breastfeed him, but he is too sleepy. We will try again later. Some in-laws came to visit. I was too tired to entertain. I tried to move and was that a surprise. I had missed the other medical procedures performed in the excitement process. What had happened to me? Surprise, surprise! Morning rolls around the next day and I am asked to get up and walk and take sitz baths at least twice a day. I thought to myself, "are you people insane?" How can I do any of this? But after the first and second day, I felt human again. The whole ordeal of delivery finally begins to fade from memory.

I slept a lot; the baby slept a lot and Doc finally got some much-needed sleep. We did not go home for about five days. The baby was jaundiced and the valve in his heart was not yet closed. He was premature and had to be incubated. He is quite sleepy until the ride home. The cold December air hit him, and he screamed all the way home. My immediate reaction was to say, "let's take him back to the doctor, something is very wrong." We thought that we were well prepared. Two college educated people. We had taken classes on birthing, lactation, the works. How hard could it be to care for one little person? We quickly realized that we were neophytes.

Preface

This book is about the death of our only son and our eldest child at the early age of 28. Chapters discuss topics exploring reactions to loss and how each loss evokes similar yet different emotions. Despite the universality of the loss of a loved one, experiences of grief and bereavement are similar for those left behind yet can differ by age, gender and other aspects of life and culture. The contributors to chapters in this book are of all ages, denominations, ethnicities, genders, and races. Each chapter closes with brief sections titled *Make Every Moment Matter, Spiritual Encouragement, Practical ways to Support those who Grieve, and Next Steps. Make Every Moment Matter* presents suggestions on how to honor your loved one's life and how you might gain and lend support to others who are suffering or have suffered loss. *Spiritual Encouragement* and *Practical ways to Support those who Grieve* are self-explanatory. The section on *Next Steps* asks us to contemplate what immediate steps we will take to ensure that there is ongoing emphasis on how one can get through this phenomenon called grief that we cannot escape.

We, my family and I, chose to make something valuable and positive out of a devastating tragedy. Our endeavors are not intended just for ourselves, but for others who have experienced the same heartbreaks. We are so thankful to those who reached out to us upon the occasion of our loss. We realized that for too long we have witnessed people walking around like empty shells of themselves following the loss of a loved one. Their losses seemed to have devastated them to the point of being paralyzed in their grief. Witnessing the experiences of our loss in the context of others caused us to be sensitive to their not realizing that there is hope for the weary and the burdened. The memories, thoughts and aspirations expressed in these writings are from personal experiences in our own family, counseling with others about their respective losses, and information based on authentic research about the diverse topics covered. Our hope is that this book will help others who are grieving. Those who might experience grief for whom we are writing include parents, grandparents, aunts, uncles, siblings, spouses, pet owners, friends, and significant others. We recognize that in life all of us cope in our own way with the loss of our loved one, no matter the age or circumstance. In the initial pages you read about the birth, life, and death of a young man with a bright and promising future. Those left behind; his father, mother, and two sisters honor his memory by living life to the fullest in his name. *We Are Making Every Moment Matter.*

It is my prayer that this little book helps readers to appreciate that our sufferings because of loss can propel us to greater healing. We will also pinpoint how our own spirituality helps us to make the best of life after loss. We can emerge from tragedy stronger than before the tragedy took place. It will take a multidimensional approach and considerable inner strength to grow into a life of satisfaction for those who are still living after a loved one transitions into the *afterlife.*

This book is like no other account; the death of a child and many other types of death are important because no two accounts are the same. Reactions vary from family to family, parent to parent, sibling to sibling, grandparents, uncles, aunts, cousins, and friends. When a loss occurs (particularly when the loss is a death) decisions need to be made quickly afterwards... How are we going to react? How will we be able to go on and live a fulfilling life? Loss causes us to lose equilibrium. Although we suffer losses of many kinds, we never quite fully get the knack for handling losses by the death of a loved one that we suffer.

No one has the secret to encountering loss and understanding how death will affect us. If we are believers, our faith helps us to deal with the loss. But as believers we are not immune from going through the same phases of grief just like anyone else. We grieve mightily too. The difference for a believer compared to that of a nonbeliever is that we have hope for the *afterlife.* Although are times when experiencing loss may cause a believer to question their faith or question God's love for her or him. Consequently, when we are in the throes of despair, we are not our normal selves. All we know is that we are in pain, and we want someone, anyone, to take the aching away. The truth of the matter is, experiencing grief is inevitable. Grief is certainly not discriminatory; it is all inclusive; every living human being will get the opportunity to experience it.

Afterlife for The Living: Make Every Moment Matter, challenges those who have suffered a loss through death to engage in concerted efforts that are painstakingly planned and consciously executed daily to live a better life. The questions we must ask ourselves are, will we live on, or will we let ourselves die, in the emotional sense, with the loved one who has passed on? As a family, we made our decision. Because every thought, activity, and course of our future has changed, we learned to not merely exist, but to live life better than ever before, *Make Every Moment Matter.*

Today we honor our son's and brother's (The Late Brandon LeNorman Strong) life. We celebrate his life by living and giving the best of ourselves, *We Make Every Moment Matter.* It is by this process that we can help heal ourselves and hopefully help others to heal that have experienced a similar loss or have experienced other tragedies.

Part 1

— 1 —

When It Happens

Child Loss

This was not supposed to happen this way.
We always thought that we would die first.
We never wanted to outlive any of our children.
The unnatural has occurred. (Bernice King-Strong)

A Mother's Perspective

We were asleep that Thursday morning on October 6, 2005. I awoke at about 6:00 a.m. feeling unusually tired. I attributed it to the previous night when we had participated in Back to School Night. I am by nature a morning person and usually leap out of bed ready for the day and the day's work. This morning felt different. A knock came at the door, and we wondered who could be calling at such an early hour. My husband went to the door. He called for me to come downstairs. I came down and saw two state police officers standing at the door. I immediately knew something was wrong. I remember saying "I know enough to know that this is not good," not even thinking that my son was involved. I do not remember if one or both officers spoke. They asked if we owned a gold Altima car. We said "yes." Still wondering why, they were asking. The male officer said, "I am sorry to tell you that your son was killed in a car accident." He stated where the accident took place, and asked if there

1

was anyone who they could call for us. I asked where my son was, and he said, "at Cayuga Medical Center." It still had not registered with me that he was dead. I rationalized that if he was at the hospital, he would still be alive.

The female officer escorted me to the bedroom to get dressed. Everything was moving in slow motion, and we were in a fog. Also, two female neighbors came to enquire about our wellbeing before we left, I did not even know their names, but they wanted to know what happened and how they could help us? The fact that he was dead did not set in until I saw him at the hospital morgue in the viewing room for the first time. I then knew that he was truly dead. Two friends accompanied us to the viewing room. The Reverends Clark from the Ithaca community. An officer known to my husband from Cornell University drove us to the hospital. After seeing his cold body lying there, I could not get the picture out of my mind. As I requested, the social workers tried to make sure he was clean and that his face was washed. I had requested that I not see any blood on him. They could only do so much, and I appreciated their efforts. Upon approaching his body, I saw a small scar on his face. The police officer had said there was a small cut on his cheek. I saw that. We later learned from the funeral director that he had a crushed chest because he had been ejected from the car and landed on a rock. His body seemed whole except for that injury. How do you unsee what you have seen and will never forget for as long as you live? The news has now spread quickly in the small upstate New York Community and members of Cornell University, Lehman Alternative School and Ithaca community came to our home to lend their support. They were so incredibly meaningful, and their presence was needed in the days that followed.

So, it began. The change that would alter the rest of our lives. Nothing would ever be the same for our family of five. We were now a family of four. We all felt so heavy and drained. Yet we somehow managed to gather enough strength, with help from friends, to decide to go to the hospital for that first goodbye. Members from our church took phone calls. Church Officers and members came over and offered prayers and comfort. So many Cornell friends and Ithaca City School District friends came. I can still see their faces; their smiles are forever emblazoned in my mind and heart.

As we returned from the hospital I remembered thinking, it was a beautiful day weather wise. Brandon loved to sit on the back porch and play with Sasha the dog, and that is where I went. To the back porch. I needed to feel his presence. Sasha was taken outside by friends. The mounds of visitors had disturbed her, and she was barking loudly. Could she sense what was going on? Would she look for him every day now? I wondered how we would manage through all of this. I could not take a solid breath. I felt I could never breathe again, let alone live to see the next day. The passing days and weeks were like a dream; no, actually it was like a nightmare. The shock of it all was so numbing to the point that I felt ok and wondered if this was an appropriate reaction to such a loss?

When this happened, my mind immediately went back to the loss of my oldest brother about 20 years earlier when he was young. His death was the first deep loss that I had suffered from a close relative as an adult. I remember thinking, this is what it must have felt like for my mother when he died. Yet, she managed his death with such grace and dignity, I wondered if I possessed whatever it was that she possessed to keep me from showing my deep sorrow and feeling a broken heart that would surely give out soon.

A few years after my brother's death my mother died after losing my oldest brother. At the time, I wondered how could all of this be happening in such quick succession? Had not my heart, mind, and soul been assaulted too much in such a fleeting period? I had resolved that losing her had to be the ultimate worst thing that I had yet to experience on this earth. Little did I know the unthinkable, unforgettable, would occur in my lifetime. When you receive word from the authorities that your child is dead, you cannot initially comprehend it. You see their mouths moving, you hear their words, but you are unable to comprehend the words that they are speaking. You think that they have made a mistake and have come to the wrong household. Denial sets in quickly. Your body becomes numb, and you cannot breathe, your head spins, and you feel faint. Your life for that moment is shattered. It will forever be that way from this moment forward. Irreparable damage has been done that cannot be repaired.

Child loss is too much for the human heart to bear. The death of a child brings with it the worst agony parents and other relatives can experience. We know that child loss happens, but we never envision that type of loss happening to us; we do not want to think about it. There is no way to prepare for such a loss. Although we may not hear of it a lot perhaps no death has not touched our family, child loss is all too common in the world. The death of a child is considered one of the most horrific tragedies that parents face.

When your child dies, not only do we lose someone we loved but we lose the dreams, wishes and desires we had for the child. It is so difficult to let go of your child even though you realize you must. The mourning stage can extend to years and decades after the loss.

A Father's Perspective

For the eighteen years since his death, my son has been with me in spirit. In my moments of reflective sadness- those times when my memories of him temporarily overpower me- I can see his impish smile and hear his chuckle. While I know that those memories are blessings, I have come to live with the pain they bring because I know that they will be with me forever.

I remember that Thursday morning as if it was yesterday. My sleep became fretful, so I arose early to prepare myself a cup of tea and to do some reading prior to starting my day's work. I heard a knock on the door followed by the ring of the doorbell. I glanced at the clock and saw that it was just 6:30 a.m. and wondered who on earth could be bothering me at such an ungodly hour. When I opened the door and saw two police officers, I immediately knew the worst was about to be cast upon me. The experiences of my years of crisis work with first responders came crashing down upon me as I realized that I was about to receive the news that I had so often had to deliver to others. I only wondered who the subject of the announcement would be they were about to share. After a few minutes they delivered the news-my son had been killed in an automobile accident.

Much of the rest of that conversation is a blur to me today. My mind quickly went to what I needed to do to support his mother and sisters... and the daunting responsibilities we would have in saying our goodbyes. Thankfully, the outpouring of love and support from friends and family, neighbors, and colleagues that we received almost immediately helped to soothe the pain.

After the grueling day filled with the tasks of notifying friends and family, providing instructions for the funeral director, and oh yes, remembering to call my boss and the office staff, I was looking forward to sleep. At about 2:00 a.m. I awoke with a start. I dreamt; I think that my son was visiting me. I saw him sitting on the edge of the bed as he had been prone to do. I distinctly remember him saying, "Dad, do not worry about me, I am okay." That memory both haunts and blesses me this day.

You see, my son and I had become good friends after years of a contentious relationship as I worked to mold him into a man of principles who would live a life of integrity in which we would be both self-sufficient and happy. Mine was parenting practice built on tough love and high expectations. As his successes began to accumulate, and his pride in himself and his generosity grew, I had been offering praises for the young man who was my namesake. His death at this point in our lives was more than a gut punch; it was a life altering shock that would require more than prayer and meditation to overcome. I now believe that the vision I had was in fact a visitation by my son's spirit to help guide me into the new reality of my life without him. My family will never know how much their love helped me to work through the pain and turmoil in which I was engulfed following his death. Upon his death, a new legacy has been built- a legacy and a ministry aimed at supporting young men to become their best selves.

Loss of a Young Child

This type of loss leads to complicated grief. Parents outliving their young child is unnatural. All the hopes and dreams lost cannot be retrieved. The devastation is insurmountable. There is the feeling of guilt for not protecting the child even though there was nothing that a parent could do. You think of things such as your child wanting you and you have failed them. You see them as cold, and you cannot comfort them. They are afraid and you cannot come to their rescue. You think that they are missing their family and wonder why they have been separated. Our secular mind runs haywire and contrary to any biblical teaching we have had. All the while we know that a young child's soul goes back to God and he or she is resting in His arms. It takes time for this realization to sink in. All you feel as a parent is enormous suffering, and no amount of scripture or kind words can alleviate your pain. Parents of young children who die, would rather have died themselves. They think there is no way to go on. The only thing that propels their rising each morning is to care for surviving siblings. On other occasions some parents are not able to be around other children for some time to come. They wonder why my child and not someone else's and they feel so guilty for having those thoughts. The transitory quickness of death amazes them. How could our child be here one moment and then gone the next? Why did God not warn us or give us time? We were good parents, and we tried our best; we are good people, why us? Parents have been known to pray to God to bring the child back because it is said that there is nothing too hard for God. Yet, we pray day in and day out to no avail. Parents have been known to lose their faith for a period after a young child dies. They stop going to church, stop celebrating holidays, and stop praying. They may become resentful of those that are living a happy life.

Most parents require professional help, a staunch support system, and sometimes medication to weather the storm of young child loss. In time the grieving parents embrace the surviving children, for the siblings need comfort. If possible, some couples decide on having another child, not replacing the deceased one, but to feel the comfort of holding another child in their arms.

Loss of an Adult Child

The loss of an adult child stings just the same but often the parents are not the ones that receive the support. Not receiving support when we have suffered a loss causes *disenfranchised* grief. If there is a spouse and surviving children, the focus is on them. We tend to forget that no matter how old a child is, parents still share an unbreakable bond with that child. If the adult child was married, parents have no say over arrangements to be made concerning the deceased. Because the parents experience disenfranchised grief, this type of grief is worsened by many losses. If there is a possibility that the family will be relocating, making it difficult for grandparents to be in touch. Adult children provide tremendous support to their ailing parents if needed. The loss of this support leaves the elderly wondering what will happen to them. Under the best circumstances, the death of an adult child is seen as out of the order of nature; parents should die before their children.

As with the grief process goes for any loss, the grief process after losing a child causes physical, emotional, and psychological pain.

Physical manifestation:

Dr. Infurna (2018) describes the pain of child loss as the *"broken-heart syndrome"*. This syndrome, although the cause is sometimes not clear, can be caused by the onset of extreme emotional experience(s). It is characterized by chest pain, and shortness of breath. Although this phenomenon is thought to coincide in tandem with emotional turmoil, it does coalesce with physical symptoms that are treated with medication. The onset of broken heart syndrome typically follows an intense emotional and sometimes physical event. *Broken heart syndrome* is more prevalent in women as opposed to men and most people who suffer from the condition are over the age of fifty. Those individuals that have previously suffered from anxiety and depression are at greater risk of developing broken heart syndrome after a loss. Studies have found that there are links to more immune disorders, and cancer, among those parents who have lost children. As a result of prolonged stress that accompanies loss, we may suffer from chronic heart syndrome that may cause damage to the heart muscles. Consequently, our health care provider may prescribe a regime of regular exercise, participation in a support group, or the practice of meditation.

Psychological Impact

The trauma of losing a child affects not only the physical being but puts tremendous stress on a person's psychological well-being. According to (Wijngaards-de Meij, et al,.2008) the psychological damage done to the psyche after child death did not heal over time. Even after a period of 18 years, bereaving parents suffered from depression, neglected self-care, experienced overall poor well-being, and are "likely to have experienced a depressive episode and marital disruption".

Research, states that "while some parents did improve, recovery from grief... was unrelated to the amount of time since the death." Studies also report that "the first year after losing a younger child, a parent is at an increased risk for suicide and everything from major depression to complicated grief" (Saltz, 2005). The age of the child when death occurs has been found to have been a profound variable that affects how parents fare after losing a child. In the 2005, study it was found that the age of the child, the cause of death, and the number of remaining children were strongly linked to the intensity of grief displayed by parents. Additionally, depression was linked to gender, religious affiliation and whether grieving parents sought professional help. Some predictors of healthy ways of helping one mange the grief process and emerge whole again, were an intense sense of purpose and the opportunity to say goodbye in the case of an anticipated death.

Social Impacts

The death of a child impacts the entire family, both nuclear and extended family. Carr (2019) states "divorce in the aftermath of a child's death is not inevitable." A child' death makes a troubled marriage worse, and a strong marriage better." Saltz maintains that there are factors beyond the parent's control, which may sour or save the marriage. "Grief, trauma, and depression impact the ability to participate in all meaningful relationships." Conversely, the death has the opposite effect on some parents. They become closer because of what has happened because the other parent is the only one that truly realizes how you feel.

We realize that we are not the only ones who have experienced this same loss; we find that knowing this still gives us little comfort. Each parent must figure out a way to go on. We get up each morning and force ourselves to breathe. Some days that is all the strength that we can muster. With each passing day we witness one day rolling around after the other. You ask yourself, "what am I supposed to do?" There is no handbook. Sure, there are pamphlets, books, hotlines, counselors, and the like that help bereaved parents cope with their loss. Even though these professionals are extremely helpful, each family experiences the loss differently and part of the healing process is the work that you are willing to put in on your own behalf.

That is the reason this work was born. This book was written to help others that have suffered loss to regain some sense of control over their own lives and maintain a sense of calm when all around you in the world seems to have suddenly gone mad. Will you lose yourself in grief and succumb to a life of sadness and subpar existence or will you honor the life that your loved one lived? Through all the complexities of emotions you will experience at the loss of life of your loved one, we must decide what type of *afterlife* we want for ourselves. We are never ready to face life as a member of a club that no one wants to be in. We realize that we will never be ready to fully live the old type of life without our loved one. So, we fake it until we regain some sense of normalcy.

Death has already cheated us out of years of seeing our child be married, have children, and have a prosperous career. Will we cheat ourselves even more by withering away and not living the best life that we can fathom? Or will we live our best life? Some may choose to do the former. We choose to do the latter. We tell ourselves that life goes on and our narrative becomes one of hope for ourselves and others; we talk ourselves into trying to live. If we believe in the hereafter and there is a place called heaven, we long for the day that we will see our loved one again.

Since the death of our son, there have been signs all around us to show his presence. The day of his funeral, there was a form in the shape of an angel that hovered over the car all the way to the cemetery. His sisters have commented that their brother has visited them and sat at the foot of their bed smiling back at them. His father has heard his voice saying, "I am alright, dad." It was quite some time before he appeared to me after all the other members of the family had had their encounters. I fell ill and I was ill for a few weeks. It was then that he came and laid his cheek against mine. From that moment on, I was healed from my illness. I had waited so long for his visit. He could not come to me until I was ready to accept it. You be the judge, but I believe in angels watching over each of us in the spiritual realm and I believe he is watching over us.

The time comes when we feel we must live out the years that our child did not get to and live those years to the fullest. The hope of being rejoined with him or her in the hereafter gives us impetus to forge ahead. We do everything we can to assure our reward of eternal life in the heavens. That is why we choose to *Make Every Moment Matter.*

Make Every Moment Matter
Spiritual Encouragement

2 Corinthians 1:5 "For as we share abundantly in Christ's sufferings, so through Christ we share abundantly in comfort too."

What part does spirituality play in our recovery process? We can use our spirituality as a conduit that propels us to seek the help of God.

9

When we are broken and in despair is when we need him most in our lives. Experiencing tragedy gives us an opportunity to prepare us for the greatest tests and battles of our lives. We must learn to take advantage of these training ground encounters. As much as we lament going through the arduous process of experiencing the death of someone close and dear, we emerge with a newfound introspection about our own strength and ability to endure hardship.

Practical ways to Support those who Grieve

A word of caution. Never tell anyone that has lost a child, that you know how they must feel. Although well meaning, if you have not lost a child, you can never know how one feels. You can, however, show love and support for parents that survive their child. Losing a child makes us realize even more how life is so precious and quite fleeting.

What will you do in the aftermath of losing a child? There are ways to cope and help yourself after a child's loss. It is necessary at times to seek psychotherapy. A combination of psychotherapy and medicine are in order, depending on the depth of the grief. A combination of medication, psychotherapy, and prayer could be a winning combination for recovery.

Following is a list of ways that we can honor our loved one:

(1) Reach out to others who have suffered the same loss. If the death was due to illness, support groups that support fundraisers for the cause.
(2) Write notes of encouragement to other grieving parents.
(3) Set up foundations and scholarships in the deceased's name.
(4) Sponsor service days in honor of activities that your loved one favored and participated in.
(5) Share your story of recovery with those that are having prolonged struggles.

What will be your next step?

_____

_____

_____

_____

_____

_____

_____

_____

— 2 —

Reality Sets In

WHY DID THIS HAPPEN TO US?

Jesus said, "I am the way and the truth and the life. No one comes to the father except through me." John 14:6 NIV

Why must we suffer the death of a loved one? Why not us? None of us is immune to the sting, tragedy, devastation of the death of a loved one. Eventually each one of us will be affected, immediately or distantly by the death of someone we knew. That person could be a son, daughter, brother, sister, mother, father, uncle or aunt, or grandparents. We ask ourselves, is the death of one loved one any different than the other depending on your relationship to the deceased. Since I have experienced the death of a loved one in all the categories, I would have to say the answer was predicated upon who the loved one was and the personal relationship with the person who had died.

We worry if we are strong enough to go on. How do we help our spouse, our surviving children, grandparents, aunts, uncles, cousins, and acquaintances? Everyone is hurting. I tried to think of them, but my own grief consumed me. I felt guilty for not being there for them. I had to learn to forgive myself for being selfish. I knew if I did not take care of myself, I could never be whole again. Not only would my relatives lose a brother, grandson, nephew, but they would lose a functioning daughter, sister, mother, and wife. I stopped apologizing for being silent, weepy, withdrawn, angry, and intolerable. I simply had no energy for it.

There is no time limit for the grief period we will experience. From our own experience, the feeling of loss will last a lifetime. There is no quick fix. No remedy for the pain and sorrow we feel deep inside. The pain is ever present and everlasting. How do we cope, you might ask? We cope by intentionally managing the thoughts in our mind. We create a "new me." After all, the old you is gone. We are no longer the mother of our child. We are now the mother of who that child used to be. Do not pressure yourself into trying to get back to the old normal or be your old self. Your old self is gone. Know that this grief journey ebbs and flows. There will be days when we can bear the pain. On other days we will be rendered helpless and that is okay.

All of us will die someday, although we try not to think of it or prepare for that day. One would think that death would be something we all would be used to by now since so much of it has happened in our lifetime. Why is it that we can never quite get used to losing someone we love? Every time it happens, we resort to that familiar feeling of sadness and loneliness that is all too familiar every time we encounter loss. Are we simply destined to hurt?

So many things cause us anxiety. We experience pain when we lose a job, are treated unfairly, get divorced, lose our home, or move away to unfamiliar towns. Although many losses pierce our soul, there is extraordinarily little loss that can compare to the agony of losing a child. Child loss happens. Globally 3.9% of all children die before reaching the age of five, which means that on average 15,000 children die every day (Dadonaite, Ritchie, &Rosner, 2013). Certainly, with the onset of mass shootings and schools being targeted where we have witnessed more loss of children's lives than we care to witness.

We do not know why we were chosen to be in the I have lost a child club. We are there whether we choose to deal with it or not. We must let the pain be felt. Do not listen to people that have not lost a child. Do not allow them to tell you how this hurt feels. Each person will feel the loss in a unique way. Learning to manage pain helps us to heal and grow toward rebuilding our lives. The agony of what has happened to us can either render us hopeless or help us to heal. Which person would you rather be?

Terrible things happen to us all. We ask the question why did this happen to us? We will never know the answer to that question. Do not spend any time seeking the answer. You will only frustrate yourself further. Put your energy into healing yourself from such a loss. Seek counseling or connect with others who have suffered the same fate as you. Try to learn all you can about services that are designed for people going through similar circumstances as you. Be about gaining support for yourself and your family. You will find that talking with others will help you to gain support. You might feel that you have nothing to offer others who are grieving the loss of a child, but you will likely be surprised to find that your listening ear is just what the doctor ordered for them.

Make Every Moment Matter
Spiritual Encouragement:
1 Thessalonians 4:13-14

"Brothers and sisters, we do not want you to be uninformed about those who sleep in death, so that you do not grieve like the rest of mankind, who have no hope. For we believe that Jesus died and rose again, and so we believe that God will bring with Jesus those who have fallen asleep in him." We can take comfort in these words. Parents, we can be assured, because of our faith, that we shall see our child (children) again.

Practical ways to Support those who Grieve:

There are no words that are adequate, nor amount of comfort that can relieve the pain we feel when we must bury a loved one. Burying any relative is hard; albeit burying one's own child is one of the most excruciating experiences of life that we will bear. How do we go on? **How to help parents?**

(1) Challenge them to press on by living life.
(2) Remind them that each of us has a destiny and a purpose.
(3) Validate their existence among the living; their work on this earth is not yet complete.
(4) Encourage others to find their purpose if they have not done so.

What will be your next step?

_____

_____

_____

_____

_____

_____

_____

_____

— 3 —

Taking Care of Business

We needed to go to the funeral home. We went there and I thought that we would see him again. The funeral director said that he had lots of work to finish and that he was not able to let us see him yet. We began picking out all the things necessary for a funeral. By this time, we are merely floating through the air. Accompanied by more friends now, we select a coffin, decide what kind of program we wanted and what day a viewing could be arranged; we knew we wanted to take his body home to Texas for the formal services and burial. Another day passed and I had a headache, and I could not seem to pull it altogether. The grief became worse over the next days rather than better. I wondered if I could even make it out of bed.

The support we received held me upright. There was such an outpouring of love and sympathy for us. Mothers from the community shared their stories with us. A woman we did not know sent us an email stating that she had lost her son and he was about Brandon's age, so they knew each other in Ithaca or certainly through school. A lady at the credit union had lost her daughter and was very empathetic to our tragedy. At the time, I could not ask, how do you go on? For truly I felt that I must have been about to die soon after, because no one could live under such pain inside of them. Then I remembered. I have two other children who need their parents. How do we help them? We are so far away. What do we do?

When your loved one passes on, whether through illness, accident, murder, or suicide, the commonality of it all is that they are dead. All the good well-meaning words of comfort do not alleviate the sorrow at the time. You are so devastated at the loss, you cannot think, breathe, or rationalize anything. Your mind goes around in a whirlwind, and you are unable to come to grips with reality. Forget about eating or sleeping. Every time you close your eyes, you see the face of your deceased loved one. You try to eat and there remains a lump in your throat and food will not go down. Your stomach churns as though any minute you will regurgitate any food that you have ever eaten in life. Your insides vacillate between hot and numb. A feeling of grief overwhelms you. You wonder how you will ever overcome such a devastating loss. You try to remember the last words that were spoken between you. You wonder if you had noticed or even felt something stranger than usual. All the days you ever shared together come flooding through your mind. You may even start with the day your child was born. You remember everything about that day. You hold on to that day.

The inevitable must be done; we must plan. How do parents plan for a child who has passed? This type of planning evokes feelings of inadequacy; the feeling is so out of the ordinary. People are asking us about what type and color of coffin, we are asked about programs, clothing that the deceased should be dressed in. You oblige the funeral directors. Meanwhile, in the back of your mind you are wondering, don't these people know that I am in terrible grief and cannot be bothered with such details? We lament needing to go over all these details. They needed to be sorted out. You are still in a state of shock, you mechanically move through the motions of somehow dealing with the tragedy. Our brain somehow anesthetizes us to the shock we have received; that allows us to stand stoically and take care of the business at hand. Temporarily we can function on some level; albeit we may feel that we are acting out some fantasy and none of this is real. One benefit of planning is that those acts help to keep us busy and helps your mind to focus on concrete things: even temporarily.

In retrospect, more than 16 years later, I've been blessed for having something to do; making plans was therapeutic although it was not realized at the time. We now see it as our final maternal and paternal act to show love to our child. How we would make sure he was dressed in his best; use the colors he liked best while he was alive. Preparing gave us an opportunity to show how much we still cared for him and hoped somehow, that he knew how much because of the meticulous care to every detail concerning his *Celebration of Life* service.

Make Every Moment Matter
Spiritual Encouragement:

"For as the body apart from the spirit is dead, so also faith apart from works is dead," James 2:6.

Practical ways to Support those who Grieve:

(1) Please do have some type of celebration of life for your loved one.

(2) The celebration should reflect everything about their life.

(3) Celebrating the life of a child is bittersweet. On the one hand, as parents you get to choose how your child will be laid to rest.

(4) Assure parents that he or she will never know this world without you and your love.

(5) Support parents in their realizing that their love can never compare to the love that they will experience in the arms of our loving Father.

(6) Draw some comfort from knowing this.

What will be your next step?

_____

_____

_____

_____

_____

_____

_____

_____

— 4 —

Spousal Loss

*You can feel alone even though you may be.
surrounded by lots of people.*

It is normal to feel alone when you lose a spouse, even if family and friends surround us. We feel lonely because we miss our loved ones. Feeling alone is common and is an expected feeling when we are grieving. As we express our feelings of loneliness, over time, some of the feelings will subside. It's tough to realize that we need to feel this pain to move on.

Losing a spouse causes our world to lose equilibrium. We are immediately thrown off kilter. The weight of the loss can at times be unbearable. As tears sometimes flood our face we wonder if anyone can articulate the pain that we feel; you do not have words yourself to express the magnitude of your emotions. Your thoughts are in disarray with every increasing thought of how life will be or how this event has changed your life already. What to do next is ever pressing on your psyche. You have no immediate answer to so many questions. Others may empathize with your loss but cannot realize your specific distress because it is unique to you.

The loss of a spouse has a devastating effect on the surviving loved one. This person had served as a lifetime companion; we feel abandoned and adrift without them. Our universe has been altered. Not only are we mourning the loss of our spouse, oftentimes we also mourn the loss of connectedness to extended-in-law family and friends. We grieve our life as a couple as an unfamiliar aloneness engulfs us. Now we are single, and we are not invited to gatherings or dinners where most couples, our friends, can be found. Understandably our married friends need to grow into the knowledge of how to cope with our new identity. Many will not know how to respond out of fear of making us feel upset. So, they stay away. They do not invite us out. They stopped visiting our home. Although we are mourning, our sadness approaches a new depth in the increasing sense of isolation that causes us to feel even more alone. For many people, the pain is too much to bear. We do not know what to say. The most intelligent people among all seem to lack the knowledge and skills to deal with grief. Grief is an uncomfortable subject that most would rather avoid rather than learn about it. It is important that we educate ourselves to walk the grief journey more fully. I thank God for the grief ministry of my church and that provided by the funeral director.

It is so important for friends and family to realize the importance of continued engagement with family and friends for the surviving spouse. The impact of losing a spouse has a profound effect on the remaining spouse. For example: frequently the surviving spouse may neglect their own health after losing their companion. Mendoza (2018) emphasizes paying attention to the issue of the surviving spouse neglecting their self-care because it can be the cause of a number of dangerous health outcomes. Their sleep pattern can be altered, their eating habits may become erratic, they may forget to take their medications on time or stop taking medication altogether. Already under stress, the psychological devastation that ensues at the death of a spouse is so intense that survivors find themselves with a reduced immune capacity.

People have been known to present medical issues such as cardiovascular problems and cognitive decline after the death of a spouse. Researchers like Infurna and Luthra (2017) theorize that "The strongest predictors of resilient trajectories [for surviving spouses] were continued engagement in everyday life activities and in social relationships followed by anticipation that people would comfort them in times of distress". Meanwhile, Shin (2018) suggests that "having a high level of education or at least one living sibling appeared to protect against the decline associated with widowhood".

Below please find the authentic writings of those who have experienced spousal loss.

EXPERIENCING THE LOSS OF MY SPOUSE, RAYMOND LEE BAKER
(Contributed by Mrs. Shirley Baker- Shields)

We as human beings know that death is an inevitable part of our lives. For surely as we are born, someday we will die or be raptured into Glory. It matters not whether we are old, young, rich, poor, religious, or non-religious.

I have experienced the heartbreak of losing loved ones over my lifetime. However, my entire world was devastated when my mother and stepfather were killed together in a tragic automobile accident in June 1992. Naturally, I was shocked, heart-broken and in dis-belief after this occurred. God's Grace helped me get through one day at a time.

Then about eight weeks later in August of 1992, I awoke to the terrible and painful loss of my beloved husband, being called home to Glory as he lay sleeping in bed right beside me. No words could truly describe how I felt that morning. I know I was in shock. I felt like my heart had broken into thousands of pieces. I could not wrap my mind around this being for real. I wanted to think that I was dreaming and that I would wake up and he would still be alive and breathing. However, that was not the case. His death coupled with me still mourning and trying to cope with my parent's death, just hit me like two freight trains colliding in my mind. I know I cried and cried and cried, and all the while I could only say "LORD HAVE MERCY: I must have uttered that sentence a thousand times. I could only think about the loss of my soulmate gone forever.

I did not want to face reality, but the fact of the matter is we have no choice but to accept God's will. I thought about never hearing his voice again, or looking into his eyes, or never being able to hug and kiss each other, or sleeping together and waking up together. I thought about how broken-hearted our three children would be to no longer have a loving supportive father to watch them finish high school, to continue to be a strong role model for them, to attend various school and community functions to keep teaching them about the facts of life. That we would never go on any more family vacations or never be able to have any more family meals together or celebrate his birthday or any of our birthdays. I guess I was selfish in thinking that it seemed so unfair for him to be gone and he was only forty-two.

I tried to recall all the happy times and memories Raymond and I and the kids shared over the years. I knew that God does not make any mistakes. I was raised to be a God-fearing Christian person from an incredibly youthful age, and I accepted Jesus Christ as my Savior. I have never doubted His love for me or the ultimate sacrifice that he died for all of our sins. I know that it was truly God's Grace and Mercy that got me through all of the days, weeks, months, and years since 1992. I can say that He is still getting me through day by day even today in 2023. HIS GRACE IS TRULY AMAZING EVERYDAY. PRAISE HIS HOLY NAME.

I hope that these few words will help uplift and give some hope to someone who may have lost a spouse, or another loved one and who might think they can't go on or it's too unbearable. I know that God can and will see you through "The valley of the Shadow of Death." You must pray, pray, pray, and seek Him. He said he would never leave us or forsake us. People think I am a strong person having endured all of this. I tell them "IT'S THE GOD IN ME." So, take comfort in knowing that one day when we see Jesus, it will be a glorious "HALLELUJAH TIME' everyday,

Fast forward several years later. God even blessed me to meet and marry another wonderful man by the name of Will H. Shields, Jr (a bonus husband) in 2008. We enjoyed eleven wonderful married years together before God called him home to Glory. Yes, this was another heart-breaking experience for me. All I can say is: TO GOD BE THE GLORY FOR HIS GRACE AND MERCY UPON ME EVERYDAY.

It Is Well
(Contributed by Sharon Walton -Shead)

If it had not been for the Lord on my side, tell me where would I be? These are lyrics from a well-known gospel song that I frequently think of today. In the Winter of 2003, my husband of 30 years was diagnosed with lung cancer. Seven months later, he passed away at the age of 55 years old. Looking back, I can recall feeling like I was on a roller coaster ride. Taken away from family, friends, his loving adult daughters, and granddaughter, his death left us all devastated and distraught.

Even though family and friends reached out to us and provided great support, the greatest comfort of all was of course God. "If it had not been for the Lord on our side, where would we be?" I had been left as head of household, sole provider, single parent, and matriarch of our small family.

Believe me, at some point a sense of panic passed through me. However, I gained much strength from Isaiah 41:10; *So, do not fear, for I am with you; do not be dismayed for I am your God. I will strengthen you; I will uphold you with my righteous right hand.* I stand on this promise today, as always.

It has been almost 20 years since my husband's demise. I have learned how to lean and depend on Jesus as my strength and guide. If you are going through a loss of a loved one … Let me recommend Jesus, draw strength from our Lord and Savior. I do! Horatis G. Spafford (1828-1888) experienced the tremendous loss of four daughters on a shipwreck crossing the Atlantic Ocean. In spite of his great loss, he was encouraged to write one of the greatest Christian hymns that many love so dearly; *"It is Well with My Soul,"* what a testimony!

<u>Prayer</u>

Lord, thank you for continuing to be my strength. I know that
there is nothing too hard for you. Thank you for your promises
and your constant grace and mercy for my family and me.
I love you, Lord. Amen

Make Every Moment Matter
Spiritual Encouragement:

"Do not let your hearts be troubled. Exercise faith in God,
exercise faith also in me." He told them: "I shall not leave you bereaved.
I am coming to you." (John 14:1-4, 18, 27).

John 14:1-3 teaches us that, *"In my Father's house are many rooms. If it were not so, would I have told you that I go to prepare a place for you? And if I go and prepare a place for you, I will come again and will take you to myself, that where I am you may be also* His words give his anointed followers throughout the centuries a basis for hope and endurance. Those who long to see their loved ones in the resurrection likewise have no reason to despair. The Father and son will not leave them bereaved. You can be certain of that!

Practical ways to Support those who Grieve:

A spouse experiencing bereavement needs a community of helpers to walk the grief journey with them. It is so vital that surviving spouses are not left in isolation that it becomes a matter of life or death for them. Some ways that family and friends can assist grieving widows and widowers are:

(1) Encourage them to get enough sleep.
(2) Eat well.
(3) Get involved in activities with others.
(4) Join a support group.

What will be your next step?

_____

_____

_____

_____

_____

_____

_____

_____

— 5 —

Parent Loss

No matter how old you are.
It does not matter how old your parents are.
The loss of the one who loved you unconditionally.
And always listened to you.
Their death causes shock and disbelief. (Bernice King-Strong)

While loss of any type is difficult to cope with, the loss of a parent at any age is an extremely challenging life event with which to cope. As we age, and as our parents age, we can expect to go through losing one parent or both. However, not all deaths of a parent occurs in old age. Some parents die young, leaving behind young spouses and children. Regardless of the survivors' age or the age of the deceased, the loss of a parent signifies a loss of a part of yourself. You were fortunate enough to have someone to care for you, guide and protect you and they were there for you to depend on. When that person is no longer a part of your life, you lose your sense of being cared for, supported, unconditionally loved. You feel orphaned. The manifestation of these feelings and their intensity corresponds to the ages of your parents and your age when they pass away. This can be true whether the death was sudden or result of long-term illness. Regardless of the circumstances of the death, children are left with a range of emotions.

Expect to go through and grow through the stages of the grief process. There are various stages of the grief process. After the passing of a parent, children will experience all the stages of grief and at varying degrees of intensity. We may experience denial, anger, bargaining, depression, and acceptance. While it is important for the grieving individual to recognize the stage of grief they are in, family and friends should be attuned to the grief that the child is experiencing and be supportive.

When a parent dies, a child experiences an onset of the stages of grief. At pivotal moments in the life of a child such as birthdays, graduation, holidays, marriage, birth of a child, may cause a person to revert to previous stages of the grief process. Additionally, death days and birthdays of the deceased cause us to experience resurgences of grief. We may find that the grief at an anniversary seems more intense than original grief. The first year of someone's death may be so filled with taking care of the necessary business that follows death that one's body might still be in shock. We sometimes need to have many around us to lend support. After the support has waned and we are left alone to get on with our lives, the second year or years thereafter can cause intense feelings of grief and being orphaned.

Under unique circumstances, a range of emotions can be felt when a parent dies. If the relationship between parent and child were strained or estranged, the survivor might have issues with unresolved anger. Therapeutic intervention may be necessary to work through these feelings of:

(1) guilt and unresolved anger toward the deceased.
(2) Relief might be felt if the parent died of a prolonged and agonizing illness.
(3) Although relieved at the parent's passing, there will be feelings of ambivalence associated with feelings of relief and guilt that may plague children.

Research indicates that psychological effects of a parent's death have long term ramifications. These ramifications are profound and depends on the age of the child, and gender of the child and of the parent who died.

Loss of a Mother

The death of a parent causes grief of various kinds depending on the gender of the parent who is deceased. The death of a mother is difficult because most children have a strong attachment to their biological or adopted mother or a caregiver who serves as a mother figure. Because mothers serve as our primary caretakers in American society, our vulnerability comes to the forefront because we feel abandoned when mother is gone. This feeling of sudden abandonment is manifested whether the relationship with the mother was good or estranged.

A mother is one of the most significant beings in a person's life. Loss of that figure renders us disabled to function as our authentic selves. The death of a mother causes some of the typical grief reactions; sadness, anger, depression, and acceptance. What makes the death of a mother so difficult to adjust to is we find ourselves unable to move forward with our lives as we maybe did with other losses. People have been known to want to die themselves after their mother died. We have trouble coming to grips with the reality of the death. After about the 12-month period, most people try to adjust to their new way of life. Often, the grief lasts much longer than the grief of other losses.

Young children suffer fear, anxiety, and confusion at the loss of their mother. Losing a mother puts the child at risk for having physical symptoms such as somatic problems, and sleep disturbances. Because a death of a young adult may be sudden, or earlier than the death of older people, it does not give the child an opportunity to prepare for what is eminent. Unlike the psychological stress that ensues that can most often be visualized, physical long-term consequences are not always predictable. Some children may withdraw from others, and some may be overly active and rebellious to masks the disturbance they feel inside. Some children try to mask the grief they feel by shutting down altogether and pretend that the death did not occur. Mother loss at times requires the help of a professional to get us moving forward.

Contributed by Sam (Pseudonym)

It was the darkest day of my life. My mother was relatively young when she passed. She had contracted an illness a few years back and had recovered. She became ill again with cancer of the colon and it came back swiftly. I thought she had more time. I figured I would be ready when the time came because we had been told that it was terminal. Still, it came so fast; nothing could have prepared me for the call that came from my sister that mom had passed. I slumped to the floor in agony and a feeling of being overwhelmed. My knees buckled, my breathing raced, my head hurt, my eyes grew dim with the tears that ensued.

I had dreaded this day in my mind for months, I thought still that death would be months away. To add to the agony, this day was a Memorial Day holiday. I would remember it forever not only as a death day but will always associate her death with this holiday. I lived many states away so I had to take a flight that would take most of the day to get home. While flying, I felt so heavy as though my feet would not carry my weight. I could not remember anything, but how my heart hurt. Memories of her tenderness flood my soul. I remembered all the sacrifices she made for her children. I remembered how strong she was in tough situations and how she protected us at all costs.

How could this be and why did this have to be? The shock of it all leaves us with a numbing effect. Moving in slow motion while the mind races at one hundred miles per hour, is how I can best describe how I felt. Somehow, I gathered the strength to move forward. The next days after the funeral were worse than before the services. The burial made the death final. The finality served to allow me to let it all out. No more trying to be strong, no more acting stoically because of my Christian teachings. I let it all out with my crumpled body in a heap on the floor. This release was what was needed to let me feel real again.

I can say that the pain of losing my mom has never left me. Supposedly with time, it hurts less. For some people that may be true. For me, the pain hurts as much now as it ever did. I have learned to live with the loss of my mother, and I am able to manage the hurt in constructive ways. When those death days roll around, I let myself sit and reflect on how wonderful she was and how lucky I was to have lived together in this life. I allow myself to feel, let my mind go blank, and meditate on how much I loved her.

Loss of a Father

Reactions to mother loss and father loss vary among individuals. According to Manly (2018) "Studies suggest that daughters have more intense grief responses to a loss". Studies also show that daughters have more intense reactions to grief than sons do. Men tend to show less emotion and take longer to process their feelings. Consequently, the delayed response to a death may hamper men's ability to accept and process the loss. All have a unique relationship with our father and mother. Generally speaking, a father signifies authority and protection to children. The loss of these attributes in the lives of children has been reported to cause both immediate and future negative trajectories. The death of a father can have detrimental effects on a child's life if he passes away during early childhood or in early adolescent (N. A. 2012). According to a study done by The University of Missouri, an anthropological scientist reported "a certain negative effects of a father's death cannot be compensated for by the mother or other relatives" (Shenk, 2012). Because of financial contributions that most fathers make to the household, the result of his death causes families, particularly children, may have a lower standard of living, get married earlier, or discontinue their education early to contribute financially to the family resources. In Shenk's study, she interviewed 403 older men and women in Bengaluru (Bangalore), India and asked about the death of the father before the child was 25 years old. One thousand one hundred twelve children were the focus of the study. There was a correlation between lower educational achievement among the group that had lost fathers, younger marriage, and less earning power across the lifespan. The effects were lessened for children at the ages of five and younger and older than twenty. The most significant negative effects were shown for those children who were between the ages of 1-15 years old.

Losing a father is a life-changing event. We can feel abandonment after such a loss, loss of support, loss of guidance, and depending on your age, a sense of larger responsibility to the family. After all, your biggest cheerleader is gone. We may feel what is the use. Because a level of protection we once sensed from our father or father figure is now absent, the abandonment leaves us wondering who we will rely on.

A daughter loses a major figure in her life when her father dies. The emotions of that experience will be felt for life. Depending on the age of comprehension, chronological age, and cause of death are determining factors that will affect the grieving process. Daughters feel helpless and will react to certain triggers in life that remind her of the circumstances of her father's death. It is especially important that teenage girls be monitored for signs of male attachment as a replacement for a lost father. A change in her personality is expected as a result of father loss. The cause of death and the timing of death of a father makes a difference in how the daughter copes. If the death is expected, painful nonetheless, it gives her an opportunity to say her good-bye (Williams, N. D.). A daughter's emotions will vary widely over the period of a lifetime. If the change is detrimental to her well-being a healthcare professional should be consulted.

When a male loses his father, it changes his life forever. Despite the fact that most adults lose their parents, the death of a father brings on emotions of sadness, anger, inspiration and sometimes relief. Men get on with their lives, masking their pain, but it exist just the same. They may throw themselves in to work or pretend they are ok. The grief emotions will erupt in other avenues of their lives. They may seem more volatile when they have been an even keel person. If they are prone to an outburst of anger, they are likely to be more aggressive in their anger toward themselves and others. However, men will be reflective about their fathers and the experiences they once shared. Not all experiences were good if the relationship was estranged. Still sons remember their dads even if the thoughts were not good ones and they were not sorry he died.

Sons spend time making arrangements, calling people, and receiving visitors. After a while all of that ceases and the reality of the loss stares us in the face. It may be year two when the grief really hits home. Most emotions experienced will be like the normal steps of the grief process. We typically remember all the good things about dad when he is deceased. Therefore, we feel guilty when we think of how imperfect a person he may have been. A father's death causes a son to be a better father to his own children if there are any. Either they do not want to be like him, or they pledge to be an even better father than their good father was to him.

Grief at the loss of a father can cause substance abuse in men. It is their way of coping with the loss. Some men do stop abusing substances without intervention because they are ashamed of what their dad would think of them if he saw them in such a downward spiral. Men become retrospective. They remember the good times they had with dad and what things they learned from him. Unlike women, men will feel relieved when their father passes if he has been sick for a long time or has a terminal illness that causes the death quickly. Although men grieve as we all do, they can move on and rationalize the passing of the loved one as for the best or inevitable as a result of certain circumstances.

Loss of father
Contributed by Eleanor (Pseudonym)

I was at work when the call came that my father had passed. I wondered who could be playing such a cruel joke on me? I immediately said, "you have the wrong person. You should be more careful when you call people and say such things." It took some convincing, but I realized that the phone call had been true. My mind goes to my mom. Where is she? Who is with her? I have only questions at this point, no answers.

Everything you are doing up until the point that you receive the news seems so important, then nothing seems relevant after you receive such an announcement. All you can think of is where is my father? It is reasonable to think that most of us are remarkably close to our mothers. They are the nurturers, the ones that model good emotions for us, and makes the world seem like a good place. I was always closest to my dad. I looked like him, had his mannerisms, thought like him; told many times, I was a carbon copy of him. He made the world seem safe to me, he would do anything for me, even though I was a married woman with children of my own, there was no fear in the world when he was around. When he was gone, my number one feeling was fear. I found myself afraid to be in this world without him. I was afraid for my mom too. What will it be like now for her to be alone? I thought, should I act masculine now to compensate for her loss? What will be her expectations of me? I do not know how to act for myself, how can I help her? So many questions.

My grandparents are still alive. For the first time, I witnessed how they seemed so vulnerable and heartbroken for the first time I could remember. My father was their only son. Seeing them shocks me into reality. I felt that I needed to be strong for them and mom. I put my feelings on the back burner. I managed to garner the strength to be courageous. I put my feelings on the shelf and conducted myself like a trooper, stealing moments away in silence in closets, under the stairs, in my office where I could not be heard. In hindsight, I am glad that I could be their shoulder to cry on. They needed me.

In the second year, I found myself more vulnerable and sensitive to the loss than when it initially occurred. Whenever someone mentioned his name or asked me how things were going, the rawness of my open wounds of grief came flooding readily to the forefront. How could this year be so much harder than the last? The shock and disbelief have worn off. Reality stared me square in the face. Even watching my children play brings me to tears. They will not know their grandfather well; he will miss so many of their first. I resolve; this is how life must be. I swallow hard and tell myself, you must forge on, he was with you for a little while and the two of you packed a lot of memories in the time you had together.

Make Every Moment Matter
Spiritual Encouragement:
Lamentations 3:31-33

For the Lord will not cast off forever, but, though he cause grief, he will have compassion according to the abundance of his steadfast love; for he does not afflict from his heart or grieve the children of men.

Practical ways to Support those who Grieve:

Being orphaned is how we feel. No longer protected. We question how we will honor their memory. We wonder who will love us unconditionally now?

(1) During our times of reminiscing, we remember the good times.
(2) We find ourselves doing the things that maybe we liked most or sometimes least that they had done, and we criticized them for it when they were alive.
(3) We spend some time being reflective about the legacy they have left.
(4) We contemplate what will be our legacy when we are gone. What qualities will you emulate now that your parents are gone?
(5) Make them proud by being the best version of them and yourself.

What will be your next step?

_____

_____

_____

_____

_____

_____

_____

_____

Part 2

— 6 —

Grandparent Loss

At some point in most children's childhood, they will experience the loss of someone they loved. Care must be taken when we explain death to children. It is vital that children be talked to on a level that is developmentally appropriate for their age group about what has happened. In some instances, the death of a grandparent is the first occasion for a child to experience death of a loved one. Throughout the various stages of human development, understanding and reactions to an event such as death will evoke various responses on the part of individuals. We will explore the reactions to loss by children, adolescents, and adults.

Childhood

Children need a brief discussion and assurance about the death rather than a long soliloquy or detailed discussion about what happened. What is needed when a grandparent dies is a conversation about death that is honest and one that uses words appropriate and concrete such as death, died, and final, as opposed to euphemisms such as gone to sleep, or resting. Children will think that the deceased will return to them if death is not explained. Incredibly young children ages 5-7 can conceive the concept of finality and know that death is not something that is reversible.

What do you say to a grandchild when the grandparent has died? The first order of business is to reassure the young child that they are not the cause of the death. Let them also know that their death is not eminent and that they will not get sick immediately and die like grandpa or grandma did. When addressing the death of a grandparent, it is wise to avoid telling the young child that the grandparent died because they were old. Children will become fearful of old age and think that mom or dad or other loved ones that are old will die soon; everyone not in their age group is considered old people to a child. A sufficient explanation for a young child is that the older person's body can no longer work. This time the doctors could not fix them. Explain to them that just like sometimes their toys broke and they fixed them and at other times their toys could not be fixed, and they had to remove them. That is what happened to grandma or grandpa.

What is helpful for a young child when coping with the loss of a grandparent is to allow them to remember the deceased grandparent. One way of keeping the memory alive is to talk about the deceased grandparent, share stories, articles, and pictures with the young child. The child, although young, will experience a grief process. Their process may look different than that of an older child or an adult when they are grieving. Children may have what is termed "delayed grief." They may vacillate between unaffected behavior or be unusually clingy and may complain of somatic illness. These symptoms will resolve on their own in most children. However, if the symptoms persist beyond a few weeks, professional help might be in order. Certainly, if your child becomes overly fearful during this period, wants to sleep in your bed if this has not been the usual practice, does not eat well, has bad dreams, does not seem happy, seek counseling for the child after having met with their regular pediatrician for advice.

Many parents are torn over whether to let a child attend funerals and wakes for their grandparents. The American Academy of Pediatrics (AAP) advises that "allowing children to attend and participate in funerals, wakes, or memorial services to the extent a child wishes." If the child is to attend the services, parents or other close adults should explain to the child what is going to happen at the service (s). Let the child know that people will be sad and may act in a certain way. You will want to have books on hand that can explain death to young children, role play, and provide comfort and reassurance to them that they are not going to die just because their grandparent died.

Adolescence

Not all age groups react the same to death. Certainly, the adolescent time is a time for rapid change upon this age group both physically, neurologically, psychologically, and emotionally. According to the World Health Organization (WHO) the adolescent is a person between the ages of 10-19 (2021). Since this age group goes through many changes, the ways in which they process grief may manifest very differently than that of young children or adults. The adolescent was more familiar with the grandparent than a younger child by the mere number of years they have been alive and associated with the grandparent (particularly if they lived nearby and had a close relationship). At this age, a person vacillates between dependence and independence as a way of detaching from one's parents or guardians. Since many life changes happen during this period in a young person's life, the loss of a grandparent may be particularly complicated. Experiencing a loss during this period leaves bare the possibility of grief reemerging as specific life events unravel. Also, at this age group, the reaction of peers to their loss plays a significant role in their grief process. With this being the case, a school setting is a main support for adolescents experiencing bereavement (Tyson-Rawson, 1996).

Adulthood

Some adults are fortunate enough to have their grandparents still with them well into their middle-generation years and beyond. According to (Fingerman, Kim, & Stokes, 2019), the loss of a grandparent in adulthood may be expected. Nevertheless, these authors maintain that this loss like other losses will result in grief by adult grandchildren. They state that "structural aspects of relationships, including gender of the grandparent, adult grandchild, and/or middle-generation parent, may affect the response such a loss elicits from adult grandchildren." The depth of emotions to the loss corresponds to many things, (1) the relationship the grandchild has with their parent. (2) The Family Exchanges Study of 2013 found that grandsons report less grief than granddaughters, irrespective of grandparents" or middle-generation parents' gender; (3) relationship quality and worry about middle-generation parents matter most for granddaughters and those who lost maternal grandparents; (4) worry about middle-generation parents matters most for bereaved grandchildren who coreside with middle-generation parents. Results highlight the intersection of gender and relationship quality in a multigenerational context.

Make Every Moment Matter
Spiritual Encouragement:

"I can do all things through Christ who strengthens me," Philippians 4: 13.

The apostle Paul declared this statement to the church in Philippi. What this means is that God can give us strength to overcome anything that we may come up against. This passage reminds us that whatever condition we find ourselves in, we should be content because we can make it through with the help of God.

The very foundation of our belief system is shaken when we lose someone near and dear. We wonder how a loving God could allow such pain to come into our lives. We wonder does He not care for us? We often ponder if there was something we did that was not favorable to Him and this was his way of punishing us. We become focused on the tragedy to the exclusion of all reasonable thought processes.

Our belief system does play an integral part in how we process and move beyond our stages of grief. We are all at various levels in our spiritual development. Individuals that are still babes in their spiritual walk will need more support than a seasoned spiritually developed person. The spiritually immature individual will be angry at God and may have a crisis of faith. The hurt will not be lessened because of the loss, but the spiritually developed person will use rituals as a way of gaining comfort. Spiritually developed individuals believe in the interconnectedness of the human, the world, and the universe (Olson & Keegan, 2013). When we can attach meaning to our lives and believe in a power greater than ourselves who is able to do all things, we then begin to accept the reality and inevitability of death. We know that death is not the end. We can overcome the loss, in time. Christ will help us, Jesus alone.

Practical ways to Support those who Grieve

- Talk to your child about death and answer their questions; those that same logical and those that are far-fetched.
- Address your child's fears and reassure them that they are not going to die.
- Remember the lost grandparent by showing photographs, performing celebrations of life and telling stories of their life through a continuum of years.
- Provide love, support, and guidance to your child.
- Offer practical support for the parents and grandchildren.

What will be your next step?

_____

_____

_____

_____

_____

_____

_____

_____

— 7 —

Sibling Loss

A sibling is a relative that shares at least one biological parent with a person. Siblings can also be adopted brothers and sisters that are legally children of someone's parent(s). Siblings play a particularly significant role in families. Some shoulder the responsibility as caretaker for younger siblings, or confidants to their sibling. When someone loses a sibling, it can have serious repercussions and long-term effects for an individual's health, emotionally, developmentally, and behaviorally. Siblings that are survivors share a range of emotions that include sadness, loneliness, and a heightened sense of mortality.

According to the Centers for Disease Control (CDC), common reactions after suffering such a loss due to death or any traumatic event include (1) Shock (2) Disbelief (3) Denial (4) Anxiety (5) Distress (6) Anger (7) Periods of sadness (8) Loss of sleep and () Loss of appetite. All of these feelings manifest themselves differently for each person. Siblings may suffer from what is termed "forgotten mourners," because they feel their mourning is not recognized. As a result, they suffer from long term depression. "Loss of a sibling creates a particular kind of "horizontal" grief in which shared histories and futures are fractured, creating uncertainties and insecurities that are often unacknowledged or misunderstood" (Sciencecare.com, 2023).

After the loss of a sibling the family dynamics will be affected. Surviving siblings' relationships with their parents will change. In addition to managing their own grief, they become helpers to parents and other siblings when managing their grief. Those who are left as an only child have no one to continue that close bond of friendship with that they had hoped to share for the rest of their lives.

Survivor Guilt

One of the most upsetting feelings after sibling loss is survivor guilt. This is normal because siblings have a relationship where they seek to protect one another. Although locale may separate siblings as adult children, this need to have provided protection weighs heavily on survivors after the loss. Not all siblings keep in close contact once they begin their adult lives. Feelings of guilt about how the relationship was maintained is also common in the aftermath.

Shared Lived Experiences

The following excerpts are contributions from those that have suffered loss of siblings.

Tommy Klop

Not sure how one starts talking about the worst days of their life, scrolling over life's coals you've done your best to keep from recooking and slowly marinating to quiet smolders towards that better part of a walking, cooking mid-life crisis. Your siblings are a glue your parents were happy to let set, in that sticky part that because and becomes our bond. Losing my brother is the greatest failure of my life. I don't like to boast, but I have a few. You would think I question the harsh words or actions I spew or bestow upon family and friends alike, and I do. The ones I said and did to him the day before he died tend to stick. We are our parents' children, roots from a tree and the apple falls pretty close when it came to my father. Ideals broadcast from the sky might as well be my Father, or God. While we went to Church on those good Sundays, I'm positive it was my Father that held sway in our house.

My mistake was I thought he knew what a proverbial timeout was, especially, given some of the recent transgressions with my crazier little brother, and how it works via blocking someone's phone number. Okay, I blocked all the other calls he made because it was a Tuesday night, and you are not supposed to be playing my girlfriend in Words with Friends. In his defense, she didn't tell me either but after I speak up, you don't get to call her a raging lesbian. Ding, you go to timeout via touch tone cell phone blocks. At the end of the day, it's the best move. It's the equivalent of telling someone, while on the phone with them to hang on for one second.... And then you hang up on them. If you haven't done it, please try it for a liberating moment. Not saying do it to your mom, but maybe you're upset and she's riding you hard... the "wait, someone wants to talk to you" ... click move, just might make her pay attention next time she goes for the low blow.

This wasn't that it was pure time-out, punishment, stop it, you did bad, sort of thing. The next morning, while getting ready for work, I was passed a cell phone that wasn't mine with some of the saddest eyes and words I'll ever hear.... "David's dead."

What will life be like after this?
Kristen Duncan Gillespie

Back in 2017 my sister had to have open heart surgery to get stints put in. She was addicted to heroin and was told she had to stop using it. Thankfully, she did and was able to have the procedure done. Fast forward to 2019. She was taken to the hospital by ambulance in September because she collapsed. We were told her kidneys were failing and they needed to get better so that she could have another open-heart surgery. Unfortunately, things took a turn for the worse and on September 20, 2019, she passed away at the age of 34. It tore me up and still does to this day. My sister and I would fight like cats and dogs but if anyone else messed with the other, that was their worst mistake! I loved our phone calls, our text mgs. Driving down the road with the windows down, music blaring and us singing at the top of our lungs. Two things hurt the most though. She gave a daughter up for adoption and was never able to meet her. Fortunately, we have since met, but getting to know her, I see my sister everywhere!!! It's a blessing in disguise but still hurts that's it's not my sister.

I went through a deep depression when she passed. I would cry by myself all the time. I'd hear a song, watch a movie, hear a phrase and it would make me think all over again about her. I ended up going to counseling because I was having such a hard time dealing with her being gone. I seriously felt like someone ripped my heart out of my chest. It's hard as can be to sit there at times and when exciting things happen to my kids or me, I can't pick up the phone and call her. I don't have one person I could talk to about anything, and she wouldn't judge me, but love me. She was always there for me no matter what and it's hard not to have that type of person in your life every day. Sorry if this is all over the place. Started getting emotional writing because I miss her every day.

Anonymous

I lost my youngest brother, David, in 2009. The strongest feeling that stuck out was anger. So much anger that it was hard to breathe.

Carmen Echols and Adrienne Strong

I remember the phone call I received at work saying my brother had passed. In that moment, I could not comprehend what I was hearing. My first thought was, "where did he go?" I was in shock. How could he be gone? I just spoke with him last night. I was numb. I don't know how I got to my aunt's house, but I must have driven in a daze. I couldn't allow myself to feel anything yet because I still had my younger siblings to tell.

After the shock wore off, I went into operations mode. Getting meals for my family, getting the program printed, just trying to do anything and everything to stay busy. I wanted everything to be perfect.

Often when a child dies, the parents are surrounded by love and support. The siblings, however, get a polite smile or soft embrace and that is all. No one calls to check on the children, they check on the parents. Siblings are left in limbo. Do we deserve to grieve?

The weeks that followed were quiet. The funeral had happened, and my brother was now in the ground. I was alone. I was not the maternal figure for my younger sibling but if they needed to cry, they cried on me. If they had questions, I had to find the answers.

Where was the continued support for us? We lost our first playmate, our first best friend, our only brother. Sibling grief hurts and does not go away, however, the support available in the world for siblings is minimal. We suffer, we hurt, we close up because the pain is palpable.

Make Every Moment Matter
Spiritual Encouragement:

"Your Father knows what you need before you ask Him." Matthew 6:8. (KJV).

Practical ways to Support those who Grieve:

When a sibling dies, the survivors lose the interconnectedness they once shared with the one person that had so much in common with them. After all, there is no one that shares, knows, and feels what it was like to grow up in that nuclear family created by your parents. Siblings see each other through good and bad and sometimes their love is more ever present than the love shared by parents. It becomes difficult o know how to support siblings that are survivors. How do you help them navigate through a malady that will be life altering from which there is no cure?

Practical ways to Support those who Grieve:

Start with small gestures. Show up! Be a listening ear.
Love them in the best way that you know how.
Talking about some of the childhood memories that you shared can be very soothing to surviving siblings.

(1) Take the survivors out for a drive, bring them comfort foods, take to a movie. Many people will be spared the experience of burying a sibling in this lifetime. If it has not been your experience and we hope that it will not be, know that losing someone so close is one of the hardest things that a person will go through in this life. Your help will make this all-encompassing ordeal more palatable.

(2) If your sibling had a spouse and children, do what you can to relieve them of some of the responsibilities of everyday living.

(3) Offer to do laundry and other chores.

(4) Offer to go to lawyers and insurance visits with the spouse.

(5) Sorting through belongings of the deceased is a dauting task. Ask if this is something that the survivors would like help in doing.

(6) In the coming days and weeks there will be many things that need attention. A grieving family will not have the interest or energy to do it alone. Whatever gestures of assistance and kindness will be appreciated.

What will be your next step?

_____

_____

_____

_____

_____

_____

_____

_____

— 8 —

Miscarriage

And the Lord, he it is that doth go before thee; He will.
Be with thee, he will not fail thee, neither forsake thee.
Fear not, neither be dismayed Deuteronomy 31: 8 (KJV)

Miscarriage, also known as spontaneous abortion and pregnancy loss, is the death of an embryo or fetus before it can survive. It is defined as loss within the first 20 weeks of pregnancy. Although miscarriage is common, it is very misunderstood and the grief because of the loss is not fully comprehended. Mothers and fathers that suffer miscarriage grieve. They may grieve alone, and their grief is usually unsupported. It is not uncommon for parents to have intense grief following a miscarriage. Many people do not know what to say or say nothing and as a result, the grieving parents feel alone.

It is difficult to know what to say to someone that has lost a child. Whether to ask someone how they are doing requires summing up your own courage. If the mother does not wish to discuss the miscarriage, she will tell you. Some people may want you to ask them how they are doing because this opens the door to dialogue. Talking about the loss might be relieving to some mothers. There are many aspects of the aftermath of a miscarriage. One aspect that is often overlooked is the physical toll the event has taken on the mother. In addition to the emotional pain experienced, physical changes such as hormone irregularity and weakened body because of blood loss. Although no child was born, the emotional rollercoaster that some women experience after giving birth is also evident in women who have miscarried. Some women will seem tired; they experience insomnia, depression, and anxiety to name a few experiences. The grief will be felt in a distinctive way. This grief may result in self-blame; conjuring reasons why the miscarriage happened because of something the grieving mother did. Because her hormones are still irregular, it will take a few weeks for them to level out, so realize that destabilization is a cause for powerful feelings of grief. If you find that certain things or people trigger your feelings more than others, it is okay to distance yourself from these people and the triggers. It is important to realize that no one can tell you how you are supposed to feel or behave. Your grief is normal, and you should not deny it. Realize that you will experience all the stages of grief just as though you are going through any other loss. Give yourself time to heal.

Make Every Moment Matter
Spiritual Encouragement:

"Blessed be the God and Father of our Lord Jesus Christ, the Father of mercies and God of all comfort, who comforts us in all our affliction, so that we may be able to comfort those who are in any affliction, with the comfort with which we ourselves are comforted by God." 2 Corinthians 1:3-5 (KJV).

Practical ways to Support those who Grieve:

Experiencing miscarriage is losing a part of yourself. You may depend on your significant other to be there for you and they may seem distant and unsupportive. They are dealing with their own grief, but in a separate way. It is critical that both parties have an open and frank conversation about what each of you are feeling.

(1) Some couples wish to try for another pregnancy soon after the miscarriage.
(2) It is important to follow the advice of the medical professional in charge of your care. Each couple should proceed at their own pace.

(3) Be sure that you are emotionally stable and prepared to manage the anxiety about possibly another miscarriage before plunging into getting pregnant soon after.

(4) A loss of any kind can evoke feelings of grief. Therefore, it is healing to find a way to remember your lost child in some manner.

(5) People have been known to plant a tree in memory of their child.

(6) Other friends and family may send kind gestures such as flowers or mementos of the pregnancy.

(7) You may keep a journal of thoughts that fill your head that you may or may not wish to share with a trusted friend.

(8) If you find your depression and anxiety are too severe to manage, do seek therapy to help you move through your grief.

(9) Sometimes, a support group is needed to help you talk through your pain with others that are going through or have experienced what you are experiencing.

(10) Your healthcare provider will be a valuable resource to put you in touch with those who can help you recover from such a loss.

What will be your next step?

_____

_____

_____

_____

_____

_____

_____

_____

— 9 —

Sudden Infant Death Syndrome (SIDS)

"Crib Death" and Stillbirth

Aaccording to the Mayo Clinic definition of SIDS, it "is the unexplained death, usually during sleep, of a seemingly healthy baby less than one year old. SIDS is sometimes known as crib death because the infants often die in their cribs." The cause of SIDS is not definitively known, but it is theorized that a cause may be related to brain defects that control breathing and awakening from sleep. Research is ongoing pertaining to this phenomenon. Researchers have identified some risk factors and cautionary measures that can alleviate the occurrence of this type of death. One such measure is to place your baby on his or her back to sleep.

Both physical and environmental factors have been discovered to be contributing factors for SIDS.

Physical Factors

(1) Brain defects. The part of the brain that regulates breathing and awakening has not developed enough to sustain the normal functions that sustain life.

(2) Prematurity. Babies of low birth weight is a contributing factor to underdeveloped brain functioning.

(3) Concurrent multiple births increases the risks of underdeveloped brain functioning in one or other of the children.

(4) Respiratory infection. Children that have died of SIDS reported had a cold, contributing to respiratory problems.

Environmental Factors

(1) Babies placed on their side or stomach for sleeping may have more difficulty breathing.

(2) Lying face down on a soft surface; causing airway blockage.

(3) The baby sleeping with parents, pets, or siblings in the same bed.

(4) Being overly heated while sleeping.

SIDS can happen to any family and any child. However, there are known risks factors that contribute to a higher probability that conditions are strong for SIDS to occur.

Risk Factors Contributing to the Occurrence of SIDS

(1) Boys are more susceptible to SIDS than girls.

(2) Infants between the 2nd. and 4th. months are more susceptible to dying from SIDS.

(3) Non-white babies are more prone to die from SIDS.

(4) Siblings or cousins who have died from SIDS, put a newborn at higher risks of SIDS.

(5) A household where residents smoke puts the baby at higher risk for SIDS.

(6) Prematurity and low birth rate increases the potential for death from SIDS.

Mingled with physical, environmental, and other risk factors, there are known maternal risk factors for babies dying of SIDS. These factors are a mother younger than 20 years of age, the mother smokes cigarettes while pregnant, uses drugs, and has not had adequate prenatal care. Knowing the risk factors and actively participating in efforts to prevent SIDS are still no guarantee that a baby will not succumb to crib death.

Babies who die suddenly when they otherwise seemed completely healthy, causes shock and intense grief for parents. The extended family also grieves mightily at the loss of the young child. The family searches for answers as to why this happened to the child. When an autopsy is performed as sometimes it often is, there may be no explainable cause of death to be found. When this is the case, medical personnel rule the death as dying by SIDS. Parents need to be aware that when crib death occurs, there will be an investigation conducted by the police. This is standard procedure. Consequently, the grief experienced by the family will be intensified. As a result of this magnification of already intense grief, subsequent reactions by members of the family may be the result. Parents and siblings might blame themselves and complicated grief ensues. Siblings may think they caused the death if they were resentful at the intrusion of the newborn into their lives.

Grandparents are unable to fully support their grieving children because of dealing with their own pain. A marriage can come under tremendous strain. Men and women grieve differently and because of this difference misunderstandings may occur causing stress between the couple. Sexual intimacy is altered between a couple when a child dies. The parent who found the child will remember images of the dead child and may have difficulty overcoming those images which in turn interferes with their healing process during the grief journey. The magnitude of such a loss is hard to adjust to. There are things that those who grieve the loss of a child to crib death can do to honor their precious little one's life.

Stillbirth

"But when it pleased God, who separated me from my Mother's womb and called me by his grace. Galatians 1:15 (KJV)

The death of a child before or during delivery is considered stillbirth. Stillbirth differs from miscarriage according to when the loss occurs. Stillbirth is considered the loss of a child early (between 20-27) completed weeks of pregnancy, late stillbirth (28-36) completed weeks of pregnancy, and late (37 or more) completed weeks of pregnancy. Miscarriage is considered as a loss of child before the 20th. week of pregnancy (Stillbirth Home, 2022).

According to *Stillbirth Home*, approximately one in one hundred seventy-five births each year, which amounts to 21,000 babies, are stillborn in the United States. This number equals the number of babies that die in their first year of life. Although this is a considerable number, modern medicine has been able to drastically reduce the number of late term stillbirths. However, this is not the case for early stillbirths. Stillbirth can have known causes and at other times it is unexplainable. The later in term of pregnancy that stillbirth occurs, the likelihood increases that causes will not be determined (*Stillbirth Home*, 2022).

Stillbirths have no respect for people. It occurs in all families regardless of race, socioeconomic status and at all ages of women. There are risk factors that are synonymous with the occurrence of still births. Some common risk factors are:

(1) Being a member of African American descent
(2) Women 35 years or older
(3) Having low socioeconomic status
(4) Limited access to health care
(5) Smoking cigarettes during pregnancy
(6) High blood pressure, diabetes, and obesity
(7) Have multiples such as triplets, or quadruplets.
(8) Suffered a previous pregnancy loss.

For parents and families where stillbirth has occurred, it is important to recognize that you are the parents, siblings, and relatives of the child. They were born although not alive, they were a living being at one time. They still deserve to be treated as such. The grief for parents is still the same as parental grief of losing a child that you had developed a relationship with. Parents held hopes and dreams for this child just like any other parents do. The grief lays bare the wounds of unfulfilled hopes and missed opportunities that will now never be shared. Parents and siblings, if there are any, need support from many avenues to weather such a tremendous storm. You ask how do we make the loss of a baby through still birth count? Read on to find coping strategies that will prove helpful.

Make Every Moment Matter

Remember that you will always be the parents of your child. When asked if you have children, the stillbirth should be counted among them. Remember that the mother will feel all of the symptoms that a woman feels after giving birth to a live fetus. The way in which you can make yourself useful are to give support. If you have suffered the same fate, contact the person, and give them encouragement. There are support groups for miscarriage and stillbirth. Put parents in touch with these groups when they are ready.

Spiritual Encouragement:

"The LORD is close to the brokenhearted and saves those who are crushed in spirit." Psalms 34:18, (KJV).

Remember to pray to your heavenly father to give you strength and a way to understand what you are going through.

Practical ways to Support those who Grieve:

Remember that you will always be the parents of your child. When asked if you have children, the stillbirth should be counted among them. Remember that the mother will feel all of the symptoms that a woman feels after giving birth to a live fetus. The way in which you can make yourself useful are to give support.

(1) If you have suffered the same fate, contact the person, and give them encouragement.
(2) There are support groups for Stillbirth. Put parents in touch with these groups when they are ready.
(3) Help with day-to-day responsibilities and care for other children if there are any.
(4) You have suffered a terrible blow to your emotional, physical, and spiritual self. It is important to make a positive impact for yourself and others around you that are also grieving.

(5) If there are other children in the family, they will need to be consoled and communicated with about the death. Do not assume that they are too young to understand that death has occurred. (6) Rely on your faith to help make sense of what has happened.

(6) If you know of others that have suffered the same fate, reach out to them, or join a support group that targets parents just like you.

(7) If you prefer, counseling with a grief counselor one-to-one will be helpful.

(8) When you are able, think of ways to remember your pregnancy and lost child. These rituals of remembrance can be done annually, on birthdays, death days, holidays, or whenever you prefer. Planting trees, keeping photo albums, lighting candles on days of remembrance; are just a few ways of honoring your lost child. Some parents choose to have another child. This is a personal choice. Another child cannot replace the one that was lost but may give parents a sense of fulfillment from the emptiness they have felt because of their loss. Parents should give themselves ample time to grieve before deciding to have a subsequent pregnancy.

(9) And lastly, support others that suffer the same fate as you after you have been in their shoes. When we give of ourselves, it makes us feel better. A family that has experienced the shock of crib death can empathize with another better than anyone can.

What will be your next step?

_____

_____

_____

_____

_____

_____

_____

— 10 —

Infant Mortality due to
Maternal Opioid Dependency

S ome of the most vulnerable victims of the opioid crisis in America are newborn babies born to mothers addicted to drugs. Statistics show that a baby is born every nine minutes addicted to opioids, (Wilson and Schiffman, 2015). Despite the Keeping Children and Families Safe Act of 2003, the preponderance of babies being born and then sent home with addicts is staggering. Child Protective Services are supposed to be alerted when children are born to addicted mothers, even though the child has been treated and is deemed ready to be discharged (Reuters, 2015). Consequently, their deaths are not due to their drug addiction, but what sealed their fate was being discharged from a safe environment in the hospital to a dysfunctional ill equipped home environment. Presently, most states are ignoring the federal mandate of reporting; no more than nine states are complying with the law and 36 states have laws that do not require health care officials to report each case. The reason most workers do not report to Child Protective Services is an existing exemption that states if the mother is taking methadone, painkillers, or narcotics prescribed by a physician, they are not obligated to report for fear of stigmatizing mothers who are being treated for addiction and other medical problems.

The United States Department of Health and Human Services conducted a survey in 2005-2006 and again in 2013 and found that the number of "newborns diagnosed with Neonatal Abstinence Syndrome (NAS) had grown dramatically from what it was a decade before". Nationally, 7 out of every 1,000 babies born were diagnosed with NAS. This research notes that the numbers are higher because not all babies are tested for drugs. Instead, they are tested for HIV and other diseases. Additionally, if a child is a vaginal delivery, typically they are not tested and are sent home within a 48-hour period.

Under the best of circumstances, arriving home with a newborn requires lots of support for the mother and the child. Often post-partum blues sets in the aftermath of childbirth, anxiety, and fatigue. Mothers struggling with these variables are ripe for drug relapse and this makes for a disastrous situation for the newborn's care. In fact, it is a preventable death that is just waiting to happen. Mothers are sleep deprived, during the first five weeks or longer due to the baby crying, feedings, diaper changes, laundry… add to this, the baby shows signs of opioid withdrawal such as crying, shaking, sneezing, diarrhea, choking and have trouble eating. A mother that is struggling with addiction is not capable of caring for an infant that needs constant monitoring, and she often relapses into drug use, abuse and/or neglect of the infant.

A well-known case that took place in Oklahoma and was widely publicized about a child being put in a washing machine while the mother was in a drug induced state, another child drowned in a bathtub while the mother feel asleep, and another was suffocated accidentally when the mother slept on top of him (Reuters, 2015). There are countless stories as heartbreaking and gruesome as you ever want to read. Mothers and babies suffer; whole families and communities suffer at the loss of innocent life that could have been avoided if the necessary precautions had been taken and the needed assistance given to babies and their mothers.

Realizing that the reported cases are what we know about, this opioid epidemic affecting mothers and resulting in infant mortality is just the tip of the iceberg. As a nation and Health and Wellness avenues we are failing our children and their addicted mothers. Babies born addicted to drugs deserve to live and should be afforded every possible support mechanism we have to offer to keep them safe. To those little angels who lost their lives at the hands of others, we love you and your little life mattered to all of us.

Make Each Moment Matter
Scriptural Encouragement:

For you formed my inward parts; you knitted me together in my
mother's womb. I praise you, for I am fearfully and wonderfully made.
Wonderful are your works; my soul knows it very well. My frame was
not hidden from you, when I was being made in secret, intricately woven
in the depths of the earth. Your eyes saw my unformed substance; in
your book were written, every one of them, the days that were formed
for me, when as yet there was none of them. Psalms 139: 13-16.

Practical ways to Support those who Grieve

Feelings of disenchantment surrounds us when we here of these preventable deaths. Our initial response to the news of a child being killed due to the negligence of its own mother or (another drug user that was allowed to be in contact with the child) is to seek revenge and call for the punishment of those involved in the death of the child. Some people remark that they knew it would end like this for the child. Health care workers blame mental health officials for not following through, mental health blame social service personnel for not doing wellness checks. There is enough blame to go around, and we all are guilty. The blood of these children are on society's hands. We have not done enough to protect these vulnerable human beings. You might say that all of these mothers deserve to go to prison, and no one should worry about them. Their lives should end just like their child's.

Hold on for a second. This is not an excuse, but more of an explanation. Sometimes the women want help, and they are made to feel that they are "*ok*"- after all they were sent home with the child, and no one came around to give guidance, lend support, or see how they were managing. If ever you have encountered a drug addicted mother that has a newborn on their own, you would immediately take the child. More than supporting mothers who kill their babies and grieve their death, we need to focus on how to prevent these terrible acts from being repeated.

1. A uniform national approach to reporting and monitoring of drug addicted mothers and their newborns for months after they have been released from the hospital.

2. Enforced mandated reporting by health care officials of drug-dependent newborns and their drug addicted mothers to the proper authorities.

3. Immediate intervention for mothers that are struggling with addiction and a treatment plan developed before being released to home environment.

4. Closer monitoring of pharmaceutical companies that prescribe drugs to pregnant women

What will be your next step?

_____

_____

_____

_____

_____

_____

_____

— 11 —

Accidental Death

Accidental death serves to exacerbate feelings of shock. After the initial shock wears off, anger may be directed at a higher power for allowing the accident to happen. Those experiencing the loss may blame the victim for leaving them (Corr and Corr, 2013). According to the Centers for disease Control (CDC) 2021, unintentional deaths are the third most common cause of death. The three most prevalent deaths yearly are accidental falls (44,686), motor vehicles (45,404) and poisoning (102,001).

Emotions felt after accidental death causes *"traumatic grief"* responses. The sudden unexpected loss of loved ones due to unintentional acts spins the world of survivors and perpetrators out of control. There is the feeling that everything is lost. The shock can be too much to bear for some people. Practicing Christians will question why God would let an accident happen to take away their loved one? Unintelligent individuals will say that it is because of sin in someone's life that tragedy befell them. The Bible does not tell us that Christians will not suffer heartache, sadness, and sorrows; we will have periods of tribulation too. What God promises us is that a shepherd watches over us and will provide everything we need: even in the midst of dark valleys (Psalms 23 KJV). We do not understand why God allows terrible accidents to happen. It is an extremely difficult theology to accept; God can do what he wants when He wants and how He wants. Sometimes, He does not wish to save our loved one from accidental death.

Accidental death comes in many forms. One type of accidental death occurs in a place where we seek medical attention for our ailments. Instead, we go into an emergency room or hospital and never come out. Accidental deaths are sometimes due to negligence on the part of those we trust to help us. This type of accident is known as medical malpractice.

Medical Malpractice

Medical malpractice is now the third leading cause of death in the United States. The definition of medical malpractice is when the act or omission of a healthcare provider causes the death of a patient. Two hundred fifty thousand deaths occur yearly due to medical malpractice. This form of death surpasses deaths due to Alzheimer's, strokes, and accidents. According to the American Medical Association (Gilmore Health News, 2023) the following six areas are some situations that qualify as wrongful death:

- Negligence by any healthcare provider employed by the hospital
- Negligence by the hospital with its staff and employees, equipment, and medical care provided
- Misdiagnosis
- Surgical errors
- Pregnancy and childbirth complications due to clinical negligence
- Errors in the administration and/or prescription of medicines

Death due to this type of negligence will require loved ones to seek help from lawyers that specialize in this type of law practice. The process will be arduous for the family that is suing, and the personnel being sued. *Complicated* grief will haunt parties on both sides of the lawsuit.

This type of grief will require that parties seek professional help immediately. The stress of dealing with such a huge matter will require a consistent treatment plan that targets stress management strategies. In addition to being stressed out, loved ones suffer from depression and anger, or even prolonged post traumatic stress disorder. We must reach out to our faith community, social contacts, and mental health professionals when we experience such a loss by malpractice. It will take all the services and resources we can avail ourselves of to get through such a cumbersome ordeal. When others are responsible for our loved one's demise, we feel that we must seek justice and retribution for such acts of negligence. The one emotion that is overriding is one of anger. Trying to keep anger at a manageable level will be one of the most daunting tasks of the grieving process.

Make Every Moment Matter
Spiritual Encouragement:

"Be careful for nothing; but in everything by prayer and supplication with thanksgiving let your requests be made known to God. And the peace of God, which passeth all understanding, shall keep your hearts and minds through Christ Jesus." Philippians 4: 6-7, (KJV).

Ways to Support those who Grieve

There is a time to comfort others who are grieving with words. Conversely, at other times it is better to be a listening ear than a talking mouthpiece. Grieving the loss of life to an accident creates feelings of *traumatic grief* both for the survivors and the person who may have caused the accident, like in the case of motor vehicle accidents and unintentional overdoses of medication.

Some people shy away from those suffering loss from these types of acts. They are uncomfortable and envision that the same type of loss befalling them. This action leaves the grieving individual feeling lonely and unsupported. The best ways to support someone grieving loss due to accident are:

1. Take on tasks for the bereaved
2. Make them feel remembered and not forgotten. Reach out to them regularly.
3. Be a listening ear.
4. Do not make empty promises that you find difficult to keep.
5. Same the name of those who died, it validates that they did exist.
6. Connect the bereaved to a support group that is outside the family network.
7. If you have the knowledge and skills, help the individual through the legal process of dealing with doctors, insurance companies, and lawyers.

8. Be aware that people may be well versed in their respective fields of work but have a limited working knowledge of how matters go in other areas of life.

What will be your next steps

_____

_____

_____

_____

_____

_____

_____

— 12 —

Violent Death

Losing a loved one is hard under any circumstances. Emotions of sadness always ensues after this type of loss. When the death is due to a violent act there can be associated reactions of turmoil when the death happens abruptly. Reactions vary among individuals. But some anticipated reactions are anticipated and are consistent among the general population. They will mirror the reactions that anyone might exhibit at hearing about the death of a loved one from natural causes or a prolonged illness. However, there may be exacerbated feelings of shock and disbelief surrounding violent death. When violent death occurs, the death is unexpected and the circumstances surrounding the death are abnormal. The feelings are overwhelming because of the shock the body experiences. Sadness at the loss of the individual can be profound. There may be disturbing dreams about the horrifying details of the death haunt loved ones. Loved ones might feel guilty and think that they could have prevented the death. Feelings of anger at the person for dying or anger at the one who caused the death. Oftentimes, violent death causes fear and anxiety for those left behind.

For several decades, the globe has been subjected to violence on the world stage. There have been mass shootings in churches, physician's offices, hospitals, schools, homes, malls; you name it. We fear that no place is safe. So much violence and loss of life has been witnessed that it has desensitized us to the cruelty of this kind of human carnage. Some children have only known this type of violence since they were born. Television shows, portray death by violence. Movies portray death by violence. Death by violence is so commonplace until it is becoming normalized. Witnessing violent acts leaves the entire country in a state of post-traumatic stress disorder. There are not enough therapists to go around to meet the needs of the multitudes that will suffer long-term mental health disorders because of these senseless acts. We hold prayer vigils, lay flowers, hold rallies and speeches, yet the violence continues. We scratch our heads and wonder what can be done to stop the madness. This evil that has been unleashed in society seems to have no end in sight anytime soon. We must act, or all of civilization is headed for a downfall.

The sting of violent death never leaves us. After the activism and speeches made by family and politicians, we are still left with long term forever grief that haunts our souls all the days of our life. Unlike other bereavement, this type as a result of violent death does not subside. With every thought and breathe, the breath gasping, breath taking, sinking feeling remains. It takes a lifetime to come to grips with such tragedies. We never do, we just forge on day by day trying to live some type of life for we must continue to exist. There are no words, gestures, or speeches that soothe the souls of those affected by such tragedies.

The Columbine Shootings as a Tipping Point for Death by Murder

Not since August of 1966 had we witnessed the senseless mowing down of humans by a single gunman at the University of Texas at Austin, where there were 17 fatalities and another 31 wounded. In April, 1999, at Columbine High School in Littleton, Colorado, two students entered the school they attended and killed 12 students, a teacher, and 20 others were wounded. Since that time, there have been so many mass shootings in the United States and across the globe. In the aftermath of this fateful day, students and families grappled with how to manage and recover from the nightmarish ordeal. Some chose to get on with life because they felt it was important. Others forgave the shooters because they felt they had no right to pass judgement on them. So many had difficulty maintaining their faith (CNN, 2018). Since Columbine, the report of mass shootings on college campuses (Virginia Tech) and schools, Parkland (Florida) Sandy Hook (Newton, Connecticut, Robb Elementary (Uvalde, Texas) and mall shootings (Allen, Texas). There have been others too numerous to name. Even one occurrence is one too many. It is incumbent upon all of us to lobby for more mental health services and severely scrutinize laws that allow people with mental health and racial ideologies to obtain military type guns that are designed for weaponry fit for war.

Although strides have been made to increase the number of workers, Mental Health professionals are too few to deal with the fallout of violent death/mass murders. It touches us all in a way that leaves us grasping with all our skill, training, and humanity to try and make sense out of senselessness. We are missing the obvious. We must fight evil with good. How do we do that? First start with prayer. There is nothing too hard for God. We have not prayed enough collectively. Whether you are religious or not, everyone should want the senseless slaughter of innocent lives to cease. The Bible gives us a guide as to how to fight principalities seen and unseen. Now is the time to work in tandem with faith communities, law enforcement, everyday citizens, and law makers to stop giving guns to people that do not need to possess them, stop laying down and rolling over to big lobbying organizations. Our civilization and lives depend on what we will do over the next weeks and years. If we keep doing what we have always done or do nothing, nothing changes. The mental and physical anguish we all suffer because of the violence that surrounds us is paralyzing. However, wringing of hands, shedding tears only servs to assuage our hearts for momentary relief.

We may delude ourselves into thinking that this tragedy will not happen to a member of our family. No place is safe, not even our own home. Yet, we are unable to, nor should we live as hermits, afraid at every turn. Humanity has lost its compass and we are out of skew with God's intentions for how man should live on this planet earth. What affects one of us affects us all for we are connected to one another by the bonds of nature. We are created in His image. No amount of separation or denial can change that fact. We must make a difference somehow, otherwise the evil that has caused this disregard for human life will continue to run rampant across the earth. It is my belief that collective action must take place to restore normalcy and decency and some sense of safety and order to everyday life. It is evident that depending on laws and regulations is not the total answer. That process has not proven to be successful in the past. It will take ordinary citizens rising up to make a difference.

Some of the suggested ways of managing your grief when violent death occurs are the same as those strategies used for coping with any death. The things you must do to help yourself manage your emotions are:

(1) Take care of your basic physical needs. Eat, rest, exercise, and distract yourself with hobbies. This is no easy task, but forcing yourself to try these habits can help you to restore some sense of normalcy in your life.

(2) Handling violent death is a tricky thing. What works for one person might not be the recipe that helps another. Find your own niche.

(3) Putting your thoughts in perspective helps. Thinking about the deceased in a positive light helps to restore favorable memories of them and takes the mind of the horrific cause of death.

(4) One's faith often helps to give us strength when we face challenging times.

— 13 —

Murder

Nothing can prepare us for the murder of a loved one. When they are murdered, we experience shock and disbelief. We feel that we have certainly reached the bowels of hell and there is no escape from this nightmare in which we have been trapped. Fear sets into the point of paranoia. We fear that the murderer may come for us too. The sensationalism of the homicide will garner much attention from media outlets. This possible constant barrage of infringement will have deleterious effects on survivors. Homicide grief is different than all other forms. There is no way to find reason for the loss. The brain becomes overly agitated. Thoughts are chaotic, trying to put back shattered pieces of our lives. Entire families are traumatized. The usual stoic supports are disarmed when homicide enters the picture. No one is left to support others as they are customarily expected to do. All feel vulnerable, scared, and confused. The grief is further complicated by feelings of isolation. There is a feeling that no one really understands.

Involvement and constant contact with law enforcement officers becomes very unsettling. Although there is contact with the police, they may not be forthcoming with evidence. They may appear to question family members as potential suspects in the homicide. Autopsies will certainly need to be performed and this procedure further disturbs the survivors of the deceased because their loved ones' remains will be with the coroner for an extended amount of time, their bodies will be cut open and examined.

The families of homicide victims may have their first encounter with the criminal justice system. The long-drawn-out process that the system requires cannot be maneuvered by most citizens. This will require the support of lawyers and other professionals to assist in achieving justice for the murdered victim. The ongoing process may feel overwhelming. It may seem like there is no end in sight. When and if the perpetrator is caught, there is a range of emotions felt by loved ones.

How are we expected to cope with homicide? With time we learn how. None of us is equipped at first to deal with such a traumatic event. There is no handbook that has been written that applies to all circumstances. You learn as you go. There are helping strategies that we can employ that help us to deal with the loss.

Make Every Moment Matter

Violent death that is caused by murder is one of the more difficult things to contend with. It is difficult to erase the circumstances of the death from your mind. There may be legal ramifications for what has happened; so much information must be gathered and so many people may need to be involved. Try not to let the circumstances of a person's death minimize the life that they lived. How can you help others that have suffered a similar fate? You are here for a purpose. One of the best ways of honoring your loved one would be to join a group that targets opposition to those that commit heinous crimes. For the sake of your loved one, do not let the circumstances of their death define their life that was lived. Their life mattered; be determined that they did not die in vain. Keep their memory alive and make something good come from a tragedy.

Scriptural Encouragement:

Romans 12:19 says "Dearly beloved, avenge not yourselves,
but rather give place unto wrath: for it is written,
Vengeance is mine; I will repay, saith the Lord."

Family members of a murder victim are consumed by anger. They focus their anger on the perpetrator, the judicial system if they believe that justice was not served, and at times, God. Their emphasis is on their loss and how it was not justified. Anger and regret are self-directed because of lack of action to prevent the murder and doing more to affect the outcome. Medical personnel are often targets of their anger for not doing more to save a loved one's life.

Anger does no one any good, but rather it consumes the pieces of our minds and hearts where love should be instead. Try to forgive yourself and the murderer. Otherwise, living life will be arrested. You still have a life to live. Each day let go of the anger just a little more.

Practical ways to Support those who Grieve

(1) Seek out a support group for individuals and families that have suffered the same type of loss.

(2) Have a memorial or a funeral to say goodbye to your loved one.

(3) Honor your loved one by pushing for new legislation.

(4) Find ways to relax, like enrolling in yoga classes, getting massages, create moments of quiet and stillness to reflect on the good memories you have of the deceased.

(5) Write down your thoughts in a journal and then let your mind rest while you distract yourself with thoughts of pleasant things.

(6) Seek counseling if your emotions consume most of your inner thoughts.

(7) Set boundaries with inquiring people and the media.

(8) Care for yourself.

(9) Seek out a support group for individuals and families that have suffered the same type of loss.

(10) Have a memorial or a funeral to say goodbye to your loved one.

(11) Honor your loved one by pushing for new legislation.

(12) Find ways to relax, like enrolling in yoga classes, getting massages, create moments of quiet and stillness to reflect on the good memories you have of the deceased.

(13) Write down your thoughts in a journal and then let your mind rest while you distract yourself with thoughts of pleasant things.

(14) Seek counseling if your emotions consume most of your inner thoughts.

(15) Set boundaries with inquiring people and the media.

(16) Care for yourself.

Be patient with yourself and do not put a time limit on your grief process. The immense shock and disbelief will be with you for years to come. Anticipate ebbs and flows. Take your time to grieve and heal from the trauma that you have endured.

What will be your next step?

_____

_____

_____

_____

_____

_____

_____

—14—

Suicide

Experiencing grief after the loss of a loved one by suicide is surely a devastating experience. The grief associated with such loss is *complex*. The scope of responses to suicide are extensive and will include the stages of grief that we progress through under typical circumstances after a death, but the grief of one a loss by suicide will be *complicated and intensified*. There may be feelings of anger at the person for robbing you of the chance to say goodbye. There is likely to be feelings of disbelief that we had no clue that the person would attempt to take their life, or we may regret that we did not do something to prevent this from happening. The answer to the question "why did they do it?" may never be answered.

Biblical teachings surrounding suicide are found in the Old and New Testaments. Church stances coupled with an unclear interpretation of what the Bible says about suicide is divisive and confusing to many. We find accounts of suicidal completion in the Old and New Testament books of the Bible, I and II Samuel, I Kings, and Numbers (Verrett, 2023). For example, in the Old Testament, King Saul fell on his sword after losing the battle to the Philistines and losing his sons. The well-known account of Judas taking his life after he betrayed Christ can be found in the New Testament. There is constant debate among Christians about whether those who commit suicide have done the unpardonable sin. This debate continues and will continue because none of us knows for certain where another will spend eternity.

The bible speaks of one sin that is not forgiven. That sin is blasphemy against the Holy Spirit. Sin is sin and no one sin is greater than the other. The good news is that God can save the sinner, even at the point of death. The focus should be on helping those who have suicidal ideation to get the help they so desperately require.

Although there is commonality among how survivors of suicide will react, each person may be affected in a separate way. The following list details some ways that survivors of death by suicide may react:

(1) Parents may feel they are to blame and did something to cause their child to feel all alone with no other way out.
(2) Siblings may have survivor guilt and may also feel some responsibility for the death, thinking they should have seen the signs.
(3) Others feel guilty and second guess themselves, thinking if only they had done such and such.
(4) Spouses may feel negligent; thinking they knew them better than anyone and yet they missed the signs.
(5) Spouses may feel angry for their partner leaving them in such a way.

Parents and relatives may blame others for the suicide of a loved one. It is not uncommon for employers, peers, significant others, supervisors, teachers, and others to be the targets of blame when death is by suicide. These people are accused of missing the signs or performing an act that may have caused such hurt to the individual that made him or her take their life. Death by suicide is hard on everyone. However, we do not always realize that we need one another at such a time. Instead, there is a tendency to put much distance between relatives and friends at a time such as this.

Suicide happens without warning most of the time. At other times, the signs are there, but are difficult to understand. Most people are not equipped to deal with the emotions of someone threatening suicide. What we can do is get them the professional support that they need. We should look for signs of depression, isolation, euphoria, giving prized possessions away, or preoccupation with death and an interest in finding means of how to kill oneself are behaviors most reported.

Suicide can be contagious. This phenomenon is known as contagion of suicidal behavior which means that "suicidal behavior can be transmitted directly or indirectly, from one person to another" (Gould & Lake 2013). Research indicates that there are factors that impact suicidal ideation and completed suicide. For example, Gould and Lake (2013) report on the impact of media, adolescents' exposure to suicidal peers, and suggest strategies for prevention of suicide contagion.

Impact of Media Reporting on Suicide.

Most research in this area has been about nonfictional reporting. Stack (2003) suggests that this reporting has been shown to have an immensely powerful effect on suicide. The more prominent the headlines, the likelihood of greater subsequent suicides (Michel et al., 1995).

Impact on Adolescents of Exposure to a Suicidal Peer

Gould (2008) found a strong correlation between exposure to an adolescent suicidal peer and subsequent suicide attempt by another adolescent. A National Longitudinal Study of Adolescent Health found that "teens who were acquainted with family members or peers who attempted suicide, were more prone to attempt suicide than those who have no acquaintances with people that exhibited suicidal behavior" (Cutler et al., 2001). Gender played a part in suicide attempts. Girls who knew someone who attempted suicide and survived their attempt, were more likely to attempt suicide as opposed to boys who attempted suicide if they knew someone who had died from suicide.

Contributed by Victoria
Why did he do it?

It was a beautiful Spring morning in May 1995. There was excitement in the air because we had looked forward to this month for many years. It was nearing graduation day. We had worked so hard and enjoyed so many good fortunes down through the years. Now we were headed into a brave new world. We had decided to attend the same university and were making plans to enter college. Customarily, we rode to school together each day, but Advanced Placement exams were taking place and all of our exams did not coincide with one another. I did not have a car, so my mom drove me to school for the last couple of weeks. We did not ride together, but we talked daily. We had been best friends since elementary school.

On this particular morning, I did not here from Chris. I thought he must be really busy, and I will catch up with him later in the day. We had just talked the night before. I saw him at school, and he was his same exuberant self; even more so. I attributed it to our impending liberation from the mundane rituals of being teenagers in high school. Finally, we would be free to live our lives and taste the experiences that life had to offer as young adults. We looked forward to this new phase of life with much anticipation.

Chris was going to a prestigious university on a full ride, and I too would go to college on an academic scholarship. He had worked hard to earn good grades, he was a star athlete, a community volunteer and he helped his parents look after his paternal grandmother. Looking on the outside, we would think that Chris lived a charmed life. He had so much going for him. He was well respected, good looking, kind, and confident, more so than most young men of his age. On this fateful day at 3:00 p.m. in the afternoon, Chris took his own life at his home in his bedroom. His death was ruled a suicide from overdose. This would be my first encounter with death by suicide. After we were notified of this tragedy, the news spread like wildfire. I am well known to everyone at school and in the town where we lived that I was his best friend. I was questioned by the authorities. Had I noticed anything unusual about his behavior? Had he talked about ending his life? Could I give any insight into why he might have done this? Was there a girlfriend and did they break up? My mind was a blank and as close as we were, I did not have an answer to a single question that I was asked. I just felt sad, vulnerable, angry, and mixed with these emotions I felt numb. I loved him and hated him at the same time for taking this way out. Could we not have talked about it; after all we shared everything with each other, even things our parents did not know about us. I am in too much sorrow to contact his parents at the moment, but surely, they would have so many questions for me.

What had been a time we had looked forward to for so many years with joy, would end in such devastation. Ordinarily, I was a confident, and strong person; I felt weak. So much took place back then and I feel as if it were yesterday. I will cut this writing short because there is just too much to say, and I am not in an emotional space where I can put it all into words. Please understand that this writing is such a small synopsis of what really took place in the weeks that followed. I did not know that almost 30 years later that writing about such tragedy would bring back such intense emotions. I still have triggers that set my mourning into motion. Holidays, graduations, illnesses seem to bring me back to those feelings of want. I do not know what I want, but there always seems to be something missing. Psychological therapy has helped immensely. In hindsight that is the one thing that has been the most beneficial to my healing process. If I have any advice for survivors of suicide it would be to forgive yourself. Forgive yourself for (1) missing the signs—if there were any, (2) not realizing that you can know a person for a lifetime and still not know their deepest inner thoughts, (3) for the ambivalence you feel toward the deceased. Long story short, Chris' parents moved away, but we keep in touch. It gives us both some comfort to still be in each other's lives. We do not speak about the whys of it all. We just love each other, and that love is what gets us through the draining hours and days when we allow ourselves to wonder, *what if*.

It remains difficult to write about suicide. When asked if I would be a contributor to this book, I did not know what or how I should respond. I pondered for a number of weeks before agreeing to share my experience. On some level, I am glad that I did share although the painful memories remain. I hope that the sharing of my experience will help another survivor of suicide realize that we must be gentle with ourselves as survivors.

Make Every Moment Matter
Spiritual Encouragement:

"Cast thy burden upon the Lord, and he shall sustain thee: he shall never suffer the righteous to be moved." Psalms 55: 22.

Practical ways to Support those who Grieve:

Strategies to Prevent Suicide Contagion

(1) When screening for suicide risk has been performed, the conduction of suicide ideation has been known to be interfered. This is done by implementing strategies that identify people at-risk for suicide and applying strategies for prevention

(2) A common mistake made by communities that are plagued by suicide(s) is normalizing deaths *(Society and Mental Health)*. Suicide is often thought to be the result of a mental health issue. Oftentimes, it can be, but at other times this is not the case. Destigmatizing mental health issues and obtaining truthful information about the causes of suicide is vital to individuals and the community at large. You cannot bring your loved one back. However, it is wise to learn all you can and do all that you can to educate yourself and others concerning this issue and the grief that will ensue because of suicide. Grief from death by suicide is a special kind of grief. It has an extra layer of complication because of the way in which someone died.

(3) If we all thought about our daily lives and our most stressful day multiplied by one hundred, we would feel the grief of suicide the same way as a survivor. It helps to focus on one day at a time. In the beginning, set daily goals for yourself. If your goals are met, reward yourself in some way. Try not to think about all the negative possibilities in the future, as they have not happened yet. Try to see your life in a positive light, believing that things will get better and there will be more good days than bad days.

(4) Although the devastation of your loved one's loss leaves you in a state of post-traumatic stress, there are actions you can take to honor their memory in positive ways. Some ways you can make the memory of their life count are listed below:

    (1) If you or someone you know is a survivor of a loved one who committed suicide, yours and their story of survival will help others suffering the grief of such a death.

    (2) If you know someone that is struggling with suicidal ideation, encourage them to seek professional help.

    (3) Help others to overcome guilty feelings surrounding their loved one's death. Let them know that they could only do what they could with the limited knowledge that they had. (4) Encourage survivors to release the guilt they feel if somehow, they can get on with their lives and not feel guilty for living life abundantly.

    (4) Be suspicious of thrill seekers. Those individuals that have not been close to you before and now appear to want to be your best friend, are looking for sensationalism and want to be in the

spotlight and may gossip about tidbits the are privy too without your knowledge.

What will be your next step?

_____

_____

_____

_____

_____

_____

— 15 —

Euthanasia and Assisted Suicide

E uthanasia is defined as the painless killing of a patient suffering from an incurable and painful disease or in an irreversible coma. In cases of euthanasia, someone else performs the ending of life by administering a lethal dose of a drug. The word euthanasia is often used interchangeably with the words assisted suicide; the two words do not mean the same. Assisted suicide as defined by the American Medical Association's code of ethics "is the act of providing the means of suicide to a person by medical personnel." The person acts on their own with a prescription drug from a medical professional authorized to prescribe the means of suicide. The practice is illegal in most countries:

The United States prohibits death by euthanasia while other countries like Canada and Switzerland have legalized the practice. Likewise, 21.6% of the US population lives in a state that has legalized physician-assisted suicide. The states that presently have legalized this practice are California, Colorado, Hawaii, Maine, New Jersey, New Mexico, Oregon, The District of Columbia, Vermont, and Washington state (McKeown, 2023). Several other U. S. states have made moves to legalize assisted suicide. All faiths offer meaning and explanations for death and dying; and try to find a place for death and dying within human experience. Religions provide understanding and comfort for those who are facing death. Religions regard understanding death and dying as vital to finding meaning in human life. Dying is often seen as an occasion for getting powerful spiritual insights as well as for preparing whatever afterlife may be to come.

For those left behind when someone dies, religion provides rituals to mark death and ceremonies to remember those who have died. All faiths hold strong views on euthanasia. Most religions oppose euthanasia. Religions are opposed to euthanasia for a few reasons. Religious people often refer to *the sanctity of life*. There are many religiously based arguments offered in opposition to the practice of euthanasia. Some argue that God gives life so only the giver of life has the power to take it away. We must not interfere in the ending of our lives, it would be wrong to shut God out of our dying, we should not interfere in the way God has chosen for our lives to end, we are only stewards of our bodies, and are responsible to God for them and we must allow our lives to end at the time and in the way God wants. As mentioned before, most religions forbid euthanasia. For example, "The Roman Catholic Church, is one of the most active organizations in opposing euthanasia." According to the Vatican (2020) Pope Francis has spoken against euthanasia. He spoke for palliative care. Whether a religion is for or against euthanasia, each person and family must resolve in their own hearts and minds whether they are comfortable and certain about ending life in this manner. Whatever choice is made, those left behind must live with the consequences of their actions of terminating one's life.

Make Every Moment Matter

We saw you in pain
Your suffering went on, come sunshine or rain
Nothing or no none could comfort you
We thought to ourselves, what must we do?
So, we took the power into our own hands
Acting out of love and at your command
We ended your life on this earthly realm
Praying all the while that you are home at peace
with Him (Bernice King-Strong)

Practical ways to Support those who Grieve

(1) When patients are living with a life-threatening disease or chronic illness, they in concert with their families will work with other healthcare professionals like physicians, nurses, hospice chaplains, and social workers. These professionals can assist patients and families partialize and break done these major decisions into small pieces.

(2) Along with these professionals, friends can help families to appreciate the uniqueness of the individual and their unique decision, whether or not agreeable to them, to end their life in such a manner.

(3) Be careful not to pass judgement. Much restraint is needed when supporting families through assisted suicide and euthanasia. Many are of the opinion that relieving the pain and suffering of their loved one is a benevolent act and see this method as a way to honor the loved one's right to die with dignity. Some support their loved one through this end-of-life ritual because they see it as the last control an individual has over his or her life. (4) They may talk with them about what final arrangements they wish for them to make. This provides some patients and family members with the comfort of knowing that they can carry out the final wishes of a loved one. This is only a brief summary of what is entailed when assisted suicide and euthanasia are involved. Most states require consultation with a therapist when these two types of end-of-life options are requested.

What will be your next steps?

_____

_____

_____

_____

_____

_____

_____

— 16 —

Friend Loss

"Those we love do not go away.
They walk beside us every day.
Unseen, unheard, but always near.
Still loved. Still missed, and very dear."
-Unknown

Not much is talked about when we consider the experience of deep grief when we have lost a friend. Often the grief we experience is grossly undervalued or misunderstood. We are getting better at helping someone who is grieving the loss of a spouse or family member, but what about friend loss. Jesus gives a glimpse into understanding how losing a friend can be very hurtful. The Bible outlines for us that Jesus had a human side and spiritual side. He felt sorrow and sadness as we do. He allowed himself to be human and, in his humanness, he loved his friend Lazarus dearly. While Jesus was away from town, Lazarus died. When Jesus heard of the death of his friend he grieved. His outward expression of grief was to cry because of the loss of his friend for whom he cared so much. You can imagine the depth of his sorrow being intense enough to bring Jesus to tears. Jesus, being omnipotent and ever powerful, at that moment experienced the anguish that we go through when we lose a friend. He was able to bring Lazarus back from the dead; thus, showing His power and alleviating his deep sorrow at the loss.

We on the other hand do not have and should not have the power over life and death. Certainly, we wish that we could reverse the sting of death from our hearts and minds when our friend dies, but we cannot. Consequently, we experience the same anguish at the loss of a close friend that is often thought of as being reserved for a spouse or family member. Not a single occurrence of death is felt in the same manner. All of us have friends that are as dear to us as any sibling, aunt, uncle, or cousin. When that person dies, our world is turned upside down. We grieve mightily. To add to the assault on our emotional side of self, is that we do not obtain the same support at friend loss as we do when encountering other loses, although the hurt cuts just as deeply. For example, there are no bereavement days given to employees to mourn the loss of a friend. There are no rituals of remembrance afforded someone when a friend dies, such as: bringing food to the home, during the days and weeks to follow or receiving the same emotional support that a widow or other family member would receive.

The death of a close friend can be a paralyzing experience. Trying to envision a world without the friend in your life causes despair. We may find ourselves wondering how to press forward. There are ways to help ourselves and others through the grief of a friend loss. The best way to honor their life and make the world know that the person not only occupied physical space on this earth and their love resided in our heart is to promote a legacy that we can hold onto after they are no longer with us. Let us *Make Every Moment Matter*.

Make Every Moment Matter
Spiritual Encouragement

"A man of too many friends comes to ruin, But there is a friend who sticks closer than a brother," Proverbs 18:24, (KJV).

Practical ways to Support those who Grieve

It becomes difficult to know how to support a grieving friend. We find that words escape us when we make attempts to console a grieving individual.

(1) Just know that the ministry of presence is often what is needed.

(2) Small gestures such as regular visits, being a listening ear, inviting the grieving individual over for coffee or dinner.

(3) Be willing to be flexible and gauge how you might help an individual through this trying time.

(4) Realize that friends can be closer than a blood relative. Their loss cuts deep and the sorrow that ensues because of their loss needs to be recognized as much as other death.

(5) Help them to think of ways that they can honor a friend after they are gone

What will be your next step?

_____

_____

_____

_____

_____

_____

_____

— 17 —

Pet Loss

As long as I can remember.
You have been by my side.
A constant companion you were.
Your loss cuts deeply
As deep as any other loss that I have suffered. (Bernice King-Strong)

People choose to have a pet for many reasons. The significant role these animals play in our daily lives cannot be overstated. Pet owners see their pets as beloved members of their family. In some ways they are as close to their pets as they are to their spouse or children. Pets serve to function as companions, motivators to keep us active, and provide a sense of purpose in life. Many people that are not pet owners or lovers of pets cannot understand the grief experienced by pet owners when their pet dies. Grief is not recognized or validated as true grief like that we experience at the loss of an individual. This type of grief is known as disenfranchised grief. According to Meiner, (2018) disenfranchised grief is defined as grief that is not recognized such as the death of a pet, or the incredibly old adult who may have dementia, or sudden death by suicides or deaths caused by drunk drivers.

Pet owners should never feel guilty because we grieve the loss of a pet. The depth of grief we feel is directly connected to the significance we assigned to our pet's role in our lives. If we lived alone, our pet may have been our sole companion. As we age, many seniors choose to have pets to help maintain a daily routine and have a reason to get up every day. Also, pets may cause seniors to stay active and get much needed exercise because they walk the pet multiple times per day. Our pet may have acted as a catalyst for us to meet other people socially that shared the same interests and love of the type of pet we owned. The danger in losing a pet is the owner may spend most of their time alone after the pet dies. This is not good. The loss of this significant one in our lives causes us to experience grief that ebbs and flows, and these emotions may last for years. Expect to feel lonely. Trying to ignore this feeling will only cause it to resurface eventually and hamper the healing process. Use your own timetable to help regulate your grief response. Others cannot tell you how to feel and you should express that sentiment to them. Afterall, you had a unique bond with the pet that they did not share. There are ways in which you can honor your pet just as you would any other family member. Rituals can help to jumpstart the healing process. When we celebrate life of any type it allows us to demonstrate our love for the person; the loss of a pet is no different. Some pets die without any warning and there are other times when we make the decision to end our pet's life for whatever reason.

Pet Loss Due to Euthanasia

The decision to put a pet to sleep does not come too lightly. Usually, this decision is made after the pet has been diagnosed with an incurable illness or sustained injury beyond repair. Whether or not we choose to be with the pet during the final hours is a personal choice. Pets are usually injected with a drug that causes them to die peacefully and without pain. Unlike human euthanasia, the euthanasia of a pet is often seen as a benevolent approach to relieve the pain and suffering that a pet is experiencing or will experience during life. The personal decision to get another pet should be made with much thought.

Adjusting to life without a pet will be hard for families, children, parents and seniors. Taking care of an animal and providing care for someone or something else gives seniors a purpose in life and much desired companionship (Robinson & Segal, 2023). During times of personal struggle, pets have been known to bring comfort. Some people credit pet ownership with being the factor that caused them to get through tough times.

Make Every Moment Matter
Scriptural Encouragement:

"Who knoweth not in all these that the hand of the Lord
hath wrought this? In whose hand is the soul of every living
thing, and the breath of all mankind" Job 12: 9-10.

Practical ways to Support those who Grieve:

Grief is not a one size fits all. The pain of losing a pet by any means is devastating. Pets are considered members of the family. Euthanasia of a pet is seen as a benevolent act. Conversely, euthanasia of a person is seen as a deplorable act by some, and we are said to be playing God. Pet loss is felt as readily as loss of a person. Animal owners and pet lovers grieve for animals as we do for people. The grief is even more difficult because it was by choice that we ended our pet's life. Those that are not pet owners cannot appreciate the support and love that a pet provides. Whether death is due to euthanasia or natural causes, pet loss signifies for us, especially seniors that most aging people are dying around us, and our death is soon inevitable (Robinson & Segal, 2023).

You may support those grieving the loss of a pet by:

(1) Allowing them to pet sit for you.
(2) Invite them to come alongside you when you walk your pet.
(3) Show them compassion
(4) Do not minimize their grief
(5) Plant a shrub in their yard to memorialize the pet.

What will be your next step?

_____

_____

_____

_____

_____

_____

— 18 —

Men and Women
Grieve Differently

G rief can be caused by the loss of a loved one, a disaster, divorce, loss of employment, mass shootings, or a big move to unfamiliar surroundings and territory. Whatever the case, grief is the reaction to the loss of someone or something significant in our lives. Grief affects people in diverse ways. Research has demonstrated the reality that men and women do grieve differently. According to Sloan (2012) of the *Harvard Men's Health Watch,* it is a well-known fact that men and women differ in their expressions of emotion. How the sexes grieve is one way in which these emotions might be witnessed. Whether grief is due to other losses or the loss of a loved one, there are noticeable gender differences in how each manages the grief process. For the sake of this writing, we will focus on grief after the loss of a loved one.

Research suggests that men more than women tend to grieve in isolation. Men may even try to work out their grief by working long hours, or cry silently to themselves. Men also are more susceptible to substance abuse and suicidal ideation and completion after the loss of a spouse (2012). Men may have the tendency to take charge, plan after a death, deal with insurance companies, and appearing to get on with life. One distinguishing characteristics as a reaction to grief due to death is, men will feel relieved when a loved one dies if death ended a period of suffering for the individual.

Men also are known to remarry more quickly than women after the death of their spouse.

Women on the other hand, show their grief in a different manner. While these characteristics are generalizations and not all women or men will follow this pattern, more often than not, these are the attributes we notice in each of the sexes as we observe the grief process. Women are more likely than men to seek support when they are grieving. This support might be in the form of talking to friends and other relatives or seeking professional support from a therapist. Women tend to tell their stories repeatedly. They may visit or have multiple activities to honor their loved one. Women often do not feel relieved or will not voice this sentiment when a loved one dies; even if death was inevitable and the loved one was suffering.

Research states (Kunde, 2016) that women are more sympathetic to those who are grieving. They are more communicative and lend support to other men and women who are grieving as opposed to men who neither support other men or women.

Make Every Moment Matter

Practical ways to Support those who Grieve

We need to educate ourselves about the different forms and methods of grieving. Being knowledgeable about this information enables us to support all genders through the grieving process. We may have held previous assumptions about the way in which someone reacted after the loss of a loved one. Armed with this newfound information of which you have been made aware, it becomes necessary that we govern ourselves in alternative methods than the ways we previously passed judgment when we witnessed the grief process for men and women and how these processes differ by gender.

(1) Know that women have a need to revisit the circumstances of their oved one's death.
(2) Realize that men do not rehash circumstances of the death.
(3) Women need to attend numerous services that celebrate life of the deceased.
(4) Men tend to visit gravesites.
(5) Men work out their grief by engaging in physical activities

(6) Women openly express their grief by crying or seeking support from others.

What will be your next step?

_____

_____

_____

_____

_____

_____

_____

— 19 —

Grief Among Special Populations

The Lord said to him, "Who gave human beings their mouths?
Who makes them deaf or mute? Who gives them sight or makes
them blind? Is it not I, the Lord? 12 Now go; I will help you speak
and will teach you what to say." Exodus 4: 11-12 (KJV)

Moses was not a man of eloquent speech. God told him to go, and he would help him to speak without the stuttering he exhibited when speaking. There are two schools of thought concerning disabilities. In the Old Testament, some thought that people with special needs were cursed because of some sin committed. Likewise, the New Testament also suggests the theory of sin and the connectedness to disability. In John 1 9:3 (KJV) the disciples ask Jesus "Rabbi, who sinned, this man or his parents, that he was born blind?"

However, throughout later years, biblical theological perspectives have centered on some opposition to this deduction. A disabled person is not only one who possess visible physical disabled attributes but includes those who are ignorant and lack understanding about God's word. For example, the Bible speaks metaphorically about disabilities: in Matthew 15:14 it is written, "Let them alone; they are blind guides. And if the blind lead the blind, both will fall into a pit." Psalms 139: 16 (KJV) states that all creatures who are born come from God. We are unique in our capabilities and all precious in his sight. People with disabilities are to be treated with dignity and respect rather than outcasts. There are increasing laws to protect those with disabilities from ill treatment and to ensure that they are educated to the fullest extent that they are capable.

Which begs the question; should we discuss death with a person that has a disability, and specifically those determined to have an intellectual disability (ID)? There is no question that people with intellectual disabilities form strong bonds with loved ones and friends. Therefore, it would make sense that they will feel grief at the death of that loved one as well. To leave them wondering what happened without some explanation when that person is no longer present causes them to experience disenfranchised grief and further marginalizes their emotional existence. It is also a widely held view that those with intellectual disabilities should be protected from the existence of death (Forrester-Jones, 2013). Many view the absence of a discussion with those determined to be intellectually disabled about death as a benevolent act. We do not wish to upset them unnecessarily, cause them pain, or believe that they will not understand. Understandably a discussion of this type is not easy. Just remember, not involving the person with ID in an opportunity to say goodbye or to grieve a loss robs them of their right to live and experience life as normally as possible. People with ID need to understand that they will be taken care of. Also, opportunities must be given for them to ask questions about what has happened. An open and caring conversation about death with concrete examples is helpful at times before a death occurs.

The use of Euphemisms about death are not advised. Using words like gone away, fallen asleep, in a better place clouds the issue of finality. These phrases will lead the individual to think that the person may wake up, return, or ask if they can go to this better place to see their oved one. By all means use sensitivity when talking about death to a person with ID. Tuffrey-Wijne (2012), have named several resources that lend themselves to help with discussing death when dealing with people with ID: One such resource is "When Somebody Dies by Books Beyond Words. "These books tell stories in picture form to assist those with learning and communication difficulties explore their own experiences."

Make Every Moment Matter
Spiritual Encouragement:

And I will lead the blind in a way that they do not know,
in paths that they have not known
I will guide them.
I will turn the darkness before them into light,
the rough places into level ground.
These are the things I do,
and I do not forsake them. Isaiah 42: 16 (KJV)

God created all mankind. Those individuals who have special needs are as valuable in his sight as the very abled. The important thing to remember is that those who have intellectual disabilities, or any form of limiting conditions breathe, feel, and hurt like everyone else. When a loved one dies, we should be sensitive to the needs of those considered to be a member of a special population. It is our God given duty to care for all persons. We are to bear the burdens and bind up the wounds of our brothers and sisters hearts. The members of our special needs populations fit into that category.

Practical ways to Support those who Grieve

For more information on how to talk to a member of a special needs category about the death of a loved one, please consult, ManagingGriefBetterwww.intellectualdisability.info/mentalhealth/.and/ or, podcast on Spotify.com. Dr. Bernice N. King-Strong, Understanding Grief.

What will be your next step?

_____

_____

_____

_____

_____

_____

— 20 —

Cultural Responses to Loss

G rief is experienced by everyone in a unique way and is a response to loss. According to Doka & Davidson (2001) The most intense period of intense emotion can be expected in the first two years succeeding the loss. After a two-year period, less intense emotions may be felt. Also, during this time, intense emotions of grief may reemerge when looking at photographs, attending dedicated events, and death days of the deceased. Grief is counted as one of the challenging heartaches of life that we will encounter.

Although there are similarities among all aspects of the grief process regardless of the individual experiencing it, there are distinct cultural differences in the way we respond to the grief process. As mentioned earlier, there are universal responses to grief and loss that are experienced, however, "cultural expressions of grief are predicated on cultural beliefs, mores, norms, and restrictions regarding responses to grief" (Munoz & Luckman, 2004). Increasingly, some customs are changing among various cultures because of the influence of technology and the vast migration of people around the world. Although within a certain cultural group there are variations in belief and the grief response, there are key factors that influence one's grief process. Some of the indicators that influence grief responses among cultures are age, gender, family traditions and customs, faith foundations, educational background, economic status, and prior experience with death and loss (Allegra Solutions). The goal is to recognize and provide care relative to each culture as necessary (Corr & Corr, 2013). Outlined below are some examples of the cultural expressions of grief for major cultures residing in the United States. These cultural aspects are not listed in any order of importance but instead, they are listed in alphabetical order.

African Culture

As with the Indigenous tribes of the U. S., Africans constitute large groups of people from a wide variety of ethnic, cultural, and religious backgrounds. Therefore, it is difficult to elucidate the varying responses to bereavement and grief that are displayed by members of this group. However, there is a sense of community and sharing of strong beliefs about spirituality. These beliefs in spirituality in turn helps to alleviate the harshness of the grief process (Corr & Corr. 2013; Doka, 2003).

Muslims come from many different countries of the world and believe in one God, Allah. Muslims believe in an afterlife, and they call this Akhirah. Believing in Akhirah encourages Muslims to be responsible for their actions while living because they will be held accountable for these actions by God. Muslims believe that life is a test, but they will not be tested beyond what they can bear. In the afterlife, Muslims believe that the soul enters Barzakh, a state of waiting until the Day of Judgement. Muslims believe that they get to paradise by living a religious life. Reactions to grief may vary among Muslims depending on their country of origin, but burial rites are the same. Muslims may openly weep while others are stoic in their response to death. Muslims look upon death as a transition from this earth to the next world and eternal life.

African American Culture

According to Laurie & Niemeyer (2008), African Americans report more levels of complicated grief than Caucasians. African Americans have a strong continuing bond with the deceased. African Americans talked less about their grief experience and sought professional help less often than Caucasian members of society. Because of the multitudes of lost lives being played out so vividly in the media in the U. S., African Americans have a heightened sensitivity to loss, not only of their immediate family members, but members of the African American community at large.

African Americans have been reported to seek solace from members of their community to assist them when dealing with their grief. Some may rely on their faith community and clergy for strength in the immediate and long-term duration of their grief journey. Members of the African American community may openly express their grief emotions by weeping.

Asian Culture

Asians living in America make-up a diverse group of people from many cultural groups, and consequently have different modes of expressions. They tend to have a stoic response to pain and grief. Some may not express their grief openly while others feel comfortable doing so as in the case of Chinese Americans. Chinese American expressions of grief may be in concert with their religious beliefs such as Buddhism, Catholicism, Confucianism, and Taoism. (Giger, 2016). According to Corr & Corr (2013), the older person is mourned more than a child because of the loss of wisdom, and knowledge from the older individual where a "child had less opportunity to make a contribution to society because of fewer years lived". Meanwhile, Americans of Japanese descent may respond to loss by denying its occurrence and repressing their emotions of grief.

Hispanic and Latin Cultures

The term *Latino* identifies all diverse cultures of North, Central, and South America. In this culture, there are certain rules that guide the hierarchy in some families. Consequently, higher status is given to the elder male versus the younger and higher status to males than females.

Hispanics may view death to be the will of God and may openly express their grief. According to Doka, 2003; Munoz & Luckmann, 2004; Meiner, 2018, religion and spirituality are especially important for both Hispanics and Latinos. They rely "heavily on spirituality to cope with the loss of their loved one and their faith in God to comfort them in their grieving process."

Indigenous Tribes of America

There are approximately five hundred tribes of Native Americans. The largest inhabitants of the United States (US) are the Navajo. With so many tribes in the U.S. it is expected that beliefs, and traditions vary extensively among the Indigenous people. "The Navajo believe the spirits of the dead are able to take the form of natural objects such as whirlwinds and lightning" (Native American Indian Facts, 2019). Burial usually takes place four days after someone dies. During the four-day period, rituals are performed. These rituals are intended to keep the deceased spirit from trapping the souls of the living.

The Sioux (Lakota) This group of Indigenous people constitute the second largest. Tribal groups in the U. S. Their belief is that death is a part of the circle of life. These Indigenous people believe that both humans and animals enter a neutral spirit lane upon death (American Indian Facts, 2019). These tribes believe that the deceased's body should not be disturbed because the spirit lives in the body. Therefore, cremation should not be considered an option. On the first-year anniversary of a loved one's death, a gathering is held where the community, family and friends tell stories about the deceased and distribute possessions to those who were most instrumental in assisting the family left behind during the past year. These gifts may include clothing and tools (Native American Indian Facts, 2019). The way in which people of these tribes grieve is quite private.

Make Every Moment Matter

We tend to fear the unfamiliar. We ridicule other rituals and call them pagan or ignorant. It is well known that people of color tend to seek mental health services less often than Caucasians (Theriot, Seagal, & Cowsert 2003). In the United States, poverty, lack of services, disinclination to seek available resources, and perceived discrimination and hostility by clinicians are all reasons noted as deterrents for African Americans delay in seeking professional mental health services, (U S Department of Health and Human Services). It is important to be aware that "African Americans prefer self-help agencies over traditional mental health services," (Theriot et. Al., 2003).

Asians are less likely to seek mental health services than African Americans, Caucasians, and Hispanics/Latinos. They view this type of help as shameful and stigmatizing. Often there may be language barriers coupled with the belief that the community is able to do all healing. They seek assistance from informal support networks, (Spencer & Chen, 2004).

Indigenous cultures (Pacific Islanders, Native Americans, and Alaskan Natives) emphasize the protective functions of the family and community, spirituality, and traditional healing practice. Also, there is an overrepresentation of these groups in mental health residential settings than Caucasians; leading these groups to shy away from any type of aid that is seen as governmental intervention in nature, (Snowden & Cheung, 1990). Some of the known stressors among these groups that lend themselves to troublesome grief trajectories are predispositions to depression, alcohol use, suicidal ideation, and cultural isolation.

Practical ways to Support those who Grieve:

In the United States, there continues to be a rise in the number of people with minority group status. Given this scenario, it is incumbent upon mental health professionals to revisit the ways and means by which we help those in minority groups trust practitioners and help to break the impasse in their mental health access and treatment. These strategies include:

1. Advocating for insurance for these groups
2. Improving appropriateness of services
3. Providing for sensitivity training for practitioners
4. Decreasing stigma for receiving mental health services
5. Improving research about rituals and customs about death and the dynamics of grieving in each culture.

Our duty is to learn about not only our own culture, but other's cultures, customs, and traditions. We all live on this great plane called earth. Each of us bleeds, cries, grieves, hurts, and rejoices. As much as we are reluctant to admit it, we need each other more than we realize. We are stronger together than being separate. With each passing day, the world grows a little bit smaller by the minute and closer to mankind's end. Time is running out... Let us do all we can to do all the good we can. This doing good will include getting to know and understand our brothers and sister of all races, religions, and creeds while we support each other through bereavement and grief. Afterall, bereavement and grief is something we all will experience and "*grow*" through.

What will be your next step?

_____

_____

_____

_____

_____

_____

_____

— 21 —

Struggle for a Sense of Normalcy

Our family's greatest fear was that we would never be a family again and certainly we could never find any happiness again. What are some approaches you can utilize to bounce back from so much grief? There are published books and articles detailing the stages of grief and how one moves on with life. The stages of grief run the course, but it is different for everyone. After Brandon's death, as parents we wished we could have done something. Your child is not supposed to die before you do. We felt like we could not protect him as parents.

The first step in our healing process was to realize there was nothing we could have done to prevent the auto accident that caused his death. We had parented the best we knew how, and his cause of death was a freak accident that we could not have avoided. We assessed how we would move on. Mind you, this took months and years. We did not realize that things truly do not get better after such a loss, it just gets different. During holidays, birthdays, and special occasions, things did not get better, we just learned to deal with the loss in a more productive and inward way.

We were fortunate to have friends who surrounded us because we lived so far away from all of our family. Having friends nearby provided the greatest strength. Our daughters lived far away; they relied on each other for strength. What we did learn was that talking about the deceased and remembering their legacy helped a lot. Do not function as though their life never existed. Do not ignore their contributions to the family or the community. Keep remembering them in all you do. Upon a period of introspection, we concluded that we could bounce back after severe adversity and begin to live again. The immediate devastation eases after several years. The sadness and longing lasts for an exceptionally long time. You struggle intentionally to find your way back to some sense of normalcy. You learn to breathe again. We let go of some of the fear we felt about losing another of our children. We worried that this might happen again. He was so young, and they were only a few years behind him.

After this happened to us, we became acquainted with so many others that were in our club. There are people around who you never knew had suffered the same loss. When you engage more with others you begin to realize that people do overcome tragedies and move on with their lives. It is helpful to reach out to friends, and to visit with them. Stay connected with friends of the deceased. They need to talk as much as you do. They are afraid to bring up the subject for fear of making everyone sad when it helps with the healing process. To talk about the person is so therapeutic.

The fact that the deceased is the focus of the tragedy sometimes diminishes the element that they also stood for so much good in life. It is important to remember this and never let the goodness legacy die. Unbelievably, the grief will subside. It is extremely hard to believe at first, but it does come less intense over time. We are not happier than we were before Brandon died, but we can still be happy and find joy in life. Even the smallest of accomplishments seem more relevant. We have wanted to help others even more, particularly those less fortunate. We feel that those who have so much less than we do would suffer more intently because they had less resources to call upon than we did; making the mental, emotional, and psychological assault even more intensely felt. Give yourself permission to be happy again. Find new ways to celebrate life. Find joy in new hobbies or new undertakings. Make new friends and travel to places you have not visited.

— 22 —

Reinvented Normal

Life does not return to the old business as usual. If we look for that, we are fooling ourselves into thinking that time will make everything go back to the way it used to be. No amount of time resolves what has been forever altered. But life is not over. Find a way to grow from grief. We know how we have suffered. This suffering allows us to empathize with those that have suffered the same fate as we have. In our efforts to be made whole again, we find ourselves becoming more attuned to harshness and injustice.

Living a Life Full of Purpose is Possible

Some people comment that they lost purpose in life when a child, or spouse are lost. They say that they find difficulty in seeing a reason to go on. In response to this it is important to recognize that what we perceive as our purpose in life changes throughout the years. If we wish to know our true purpose, we need not look any further than the Bible. "You were chosen according to the purpose of God the Father and were made a holy people by his Spirit, to obey Jesus Christ and be purified by his blood. May grace and peace be yours in full measure" (1 Peter 1:2.) What we see as our purpose is a mere reflection of our desires and aspirations that we have deemed our purpose. Our lives have had purpose since the day we were brought into this world. Think about this meaning and we will reevaluate our self-efficacy. All things have a purpose.

Yes, the loss of our loved one has interrupted our lives. The trajectory that we built for ourselves may be altered significantly. Yet we are not to lose all focus. For this moment in time everything seems impossible, dire, dreary, and hopeless. These feelings are momentary, and the intensity will subside in time. The thing to remember is, you will get through some of the toughest times of your life and wonder how you overcame such darkness. God does not leave us alone. He is still there with us in our darkest hours. We do not always feel his presence. We must have faith that He will see us through. In our grieving moments, our faith is both shaken and tested. How do we hold on to the life purpose we once held for ourselves? We ask our father to take our pain and sorrows away from us; after all no one likes to hurt. Instead, he allows us to suffer for a while. It does not mean that he no longer loves us. If you can believe that he causes devastating things to come in our lives so that we might me made stronger, you will look forward with anticipation to the day when you can look back on hardship and grief and say like James said, "knowing this, that the trying of your faith worketh patience. But let patience have her perfect work, that ye may be perfect and entire, wanting nothing" (1: 3-4 KJV).

Nothing happens under the sun that He does not know about. Therefore, every act has a purpose whether we agree with the purpose or not. Surely, none of us can see purpose when our loved one is deceased. Why look for it? Does it change the situation at all? There will be situations that boggle our mind forever. You might ask, how do I live a life of purpose when I do not want to live life at all? Read on to gain inspiration for how this is possible.

How Making Every Moment Matter Helps Us All

We focus on our loss when we lose a loved one. We must remember that there are others who have suffered the loss as well because they loved him or her too. There are such a range of emotions that flood the atmosphere until we become so overwhelmed with thoughts running through our minds, we are unable to look outward. We become introspective because we know how much we hurt. It is hard to know or try to even ascertain what another person might be feeling.

We might ask, how can we consider reaching out to others when we can barely help ourselves? Having compassion and concern for others sometimes helps us to relieve our own sorrow. In our efforts to soothe the heartache of another we find strength in lighting the future way for ourselves. The adage, *"things could always be worse."* We do not often feel this way until we witness another's grief and bereavement. Somehow human nature has wired us to gain satisfaction from helping another person do a little better because of what we were able to do for them.

Make Every Moment Matter

There exist no occurrence, or thought, that the Lord does not know. Because he is omniscient, we can depend on Him because of His unwavering steadfastness. He will see us through all trials and tribulations. There is nothing too hard for God. If you feel you cannot go on and life is not worth living, God has the power to give you peace over all your circumstances. Pray to God because He is trustworthy to hear your prayer. Know that you are not outside his realm of mercy. God is the only one who can restore us. He is always there and sees us through every day and every trial according to His purposes. You can make your life and your loved ones count by trusting in God.

Since as believers we have been given the mind of Christ, as a gift at salvation, it is now the time that we should take responsibility to practice it. Fill your mind with the truths of the scriptures. Ask God to totally develop the mind of Christ within you. Only then will we be able to live a reinvented life that is happy and fulfilled.

Spiritual Encouragement:

The Lord has the power to transform us into people we never knew existed inside of us. We emerge as this strong powerhouse of wisdom and strength. So much so that we are able to be reflective and resilient because of what we have lived through. We have gained a new sense of commitment to human existence and condition. We have learned to use mind over matter. You can train your mind to tell your physical and emotional body what to do and how to act.

Epilogue

Bereavement and grief, and the aftermath of the two have no set timetable. All of us will experience both during our lifetime. All of our faculties are assaulted when we experience loss in our lives; the emotional, physical, and psychological self learns to adapt to loss by recognizing and accepting the loss, and/or seeking professional support. Death is not the end. We fail to exist here on earth but there is another life waiting for us once we transition from this earthly realm. There our Father waits for us just as he promised he would. Knowing this should bring us comfort. We were not meant to stay here forever. All people have an expiration date. We just do not know when that appointed time will come. For some, that time comes long after they have been on earth for several decades. For others, time seems all too short for human understanding. Know this. Everything that happens under the sun is no surprise to our Father. He knows beforehand the trials, tribulations, yes, grief and bereavement we will suffer. It does not mean that he loves us any less because he allows us to suffer heartache and pain.

At times it seems that there are those who get more than their fair share of suffering. We often wonder why such calamities befall them or their families. One of the most difficult aspects of walking this Christian life, is to observe how His followers suffer just as the unbeliever. From personal experience, I momentarily questioned why God let our son die in an unexpected and tragic way. I wondered why he took him suddenly and did not intervene to the point that he could have spared his life for a little while to allow us to say goodbye. It is exceedingly difficult to rely upon your faith when you are faced with such questions and no answers. You rely on what you know. The fact that God protects us every day of our lives. He does not leave us at any time. Even amid our trials he is still there. Psalms 23 (KJV) tells us that God is our shepherd, he restores us, he is always with us, and goodness and His mercy shall follow us as long as we live.

The account of how Christ died a horrible death is well known. Certainly, his loved ones grieved for Him. You might say, He was supposed to die; that was His purpose for coming to earth. Remember, he made himself flesh like us and he could feel the pain just like us. We all know that we are going to die at some point. The question is, will we live a life here on earth where we are striving to please God so that when our hour comes, we will be ready to die? We do things to ourselves that hasten our physical death. For example, we drink too much alcohol on a regular basis. When the doctor diagnoses us with cirrhosis of the liver, we wonder why God does not save us from death. We reap what we sow. The consequences of drinking too much alcohol is damage to the liver. Without a healthy liver or the possibility of a transplant of a healthy one, common sense tells us what the result will be. This example shows us a cause-and-effect relationship rather than God directly punishing someone because of their sin nature and as a result they died.

God, being omnipotent and omnipresent can protect us from death when and how He wants to. Does He always keep dreadful things from happening to us and our loved ones? No. We are not to question what God does. We cannot trust Him only when things are good. As believers we must trust God even when we encounter the good, bad, and ugly in our lives. We should not be surprised when terrible things happen in our lives. We are to expect them to happen. We are not immune from suffering and shedding of tears because we are God's people. Satan rules this world. However, there will come a time when Christ returns. That is the good news. God has promised us that we will see our loved ones again if they were believers as we are. The Bible tells us, when Christ returns, "there will be no pain, no suffering, no death, and no tears" Revelation 21 (KJV). The Kingdom of God will be established, and we will see our deceased loved ones. What a glorious day that will be (Hebrews 6: 17-20).

Reflections: Think about it:

How has reading this book helped you or given you the tools to help someone else along your grief journey and/or theirs?

_____

_____

_____

_____

_____

_____

_____

_____

_____

_____

_____

_____

_____

_____

_____

Glossary

Acute grief- The acute period after a person experiences a loss. Acute grief may last up to six weeks, with the individual experiencing somatic symptoms of distress that cycle throughout this time (Luggen & Mainer, 2001)

African- A native or inhabitant of Africa.

African American- are an ethnic group consisting of Americans with partial or total ancestry from any of the Black racial groups of Africa. The term "African American" generally denotes descendants of enslaved Africans who are from the United States.

Assisted suicide- suicide undertaken with the aid of another.

Bereavement-state of sorrow over the death or departure of a loved one.

Coalesce- To unite into a whole. Grow together.

Conduit-To function as a channel for the transmission of something.

Cremation-Cremation is the process of turning a dead body into ashes by exposing it to flame and intense heat.

Crib death-Sudden death of a child.

Cultural- Relating -to the ideas, customs, and social behavior of a society.

Sudden infant death syndrome (SIDS) - the sudden unexplained death of a child of less than one year of age. Diagnosis requires that the death remain unexplained even after a thorough autopsy and data collected.

Disenfranchised grief-Feeling of loss that no one understands Doka, K.,(1989).

Disenfranchised grief is a term coined by Dr. Kenneth J. Doka in 1989.This concept describes the fact that grief is not acknowledged on a personal or societal level in modern day Euro-centric culture. ...

Evoke-Bring forth, give rise to induce.

Euthanasia-the painless killing of a patient or pet suffering from an incurable and painful disease or in an irreversible coma. The practice is illegal in most countries for terminating a human's life.

Funeral-the observances held for a dead person usually before burial or cremation (Merriam Webster).

Grief- Grief is a reaction to loss. Grief is a normal response to loss characterized by dynamic, pervasive, and individual emotions. (Hospice Foundation of America, 2019).

Hospice- A home providing care for the sick or terminally ill.

Intellectual Disability- An intellectual disability is a neurodevelopmental condition that develops in childhood. It affects your capacity to learn and retain added information, and it also affects everyday behavior such as social skills and hygiene routines. People with this condition experience significant limitations with intellectual functioning and developing adaptive skills like social and life skills.

An Intelligence Quotient (IQ) test determines whether a person has an intellectual disability. IQ scores lower than seventy couples with adaptive functioning abilities indicate an intellectual disability. The severity of the condition can range from mild to profound (APA, 2017).

Lament- to mourn aloud, to cry out in grief.

Latino-The masculine term *Latino* along with its feminine form *Latina*, is a noun and adjective, often used in English, Spanish, and Portuguese, that most commonly refers to United States inhabitants who have cultural ties to Latin America. Usage of the term is mostly limited to the United States. Residents of Central and South American countries usually refer to themselves by national origin, rarely as *Latino*. Because of this, many Latin American scholars, journalists, and Indigenous-rights organizations have objected to the mass-media use of the word to refer to all people of Latin American background.

Neurodevelopmental- Neurodevelopmental disorders (NDs) are types of disorder that influence how the brain functions and alters neurological development, causing difficulties in social, cognitive, and emotional functioning. The most common NDs are autism spectrum disorder (ASD) and attention-deficit/hyperactive disorder.

Meditation- Meditation is a practice in which an individual uses a technique – such as mindfulness, or focusing the mind on a particular object, thought, or activity – to train attention and awareness...

Middle-generational- The definition of the middle generation for me is the generation that currently has senior citizen parents and are raising children.

Miscarriage- death of an unborn fetus.

Multigeneration- relating to several generations:

Murder-the unlawful premeditated killing of one human being by another

Muslim-A follower of the religion of Islam.

Narrative-A spoken or written account of events.

Phenomenon-A fact or situation that is observed to exist.

Posit- Assume as a fact.

Religion-Religion is a fundamental set of beliefs and practices agreed upon by a group of people. These set of beliefs concern the cause, nature, and purpose of the universe, and involve devotional and ritual observances. They also often contain a moral code governing the conduct of human affairs.

Ruminate- to go over in the mind repeatedly and often casually or slowly.

Stillbirth-Stillbirth is when a baby passes away before or during delivery.

Syndrome-any combination of signs and symptoms that are indicative of a particular disease or disorder. Two or more symptoms, characteristic, or set of symptoms or characteristics indicating the existence of a condition, problem, etc.

Suicide-the action of killing oneself intentionally.

Transcultural- relating to or involving more than one culture; cross-cover cultural:

References

American Medical Association. (2016). Code of Medical Ethics. Retrieved from https://www.ama-assn.org/system/files/code-of-medical-ethics-chapter-1.pdf.

American Psychiatric Association. (2013). Diagnostic and statistical manual of mental disorders (5th ed.). https://doi.org/10.1176/appi.books.9780890425596.

Bayingana, E. (2002). "The Church's Evangelizing Mission to the Mentally Handicapped" in *African Ecclesial Review* 5 (2002): 16-29.

Columbine High School Shootings Fast Facts. CNN, Cable News Network, Retrieved, May 2023, from: *How They Were Equipped That Day., edition.cnn.com/Specials/2000 columbine.ed/Pages/EQUIPMENT_TEXT.htm.*

Corr, C. A., & Corr, D. M. (2013). Death and dying, life and living (seventh. Ed. Belmont, CA: Wadsworth/Cengage Learning.

Doka, K. Y., & Davidson, J. D. (Eds.). 2001. Caregiving and loss. Washington, D. C.: Hospice Foundation of America.

Feigenbaum, D., Chesson, B., & Gaines Lanzi, R., (2012): Building a Network of Grief Support on College Campuses: A National Grassroots Initiative, Journal of College Student Psychotherapy, 26:2, 99-120

Forrester-Jones, R. (2013). The road barely taken funerals, and people with intellectual disabilities. *Journal of Applied Research in Intellectual Disabilities.* 26, (3), pp. 243-256.

Giger, J. N. (2016). Transcultural nursing: Assessment and intervention. (7th. Ed.). St. louis, MO: Elsevier.

Gould, M., & Lake, A. (2013). The Contagion of Suicidal Behavior. Forum on Global Violence Prevention; Board on Global Health; Institute of Medicine; National Research Council:

Contagion of Violence: Workshop Summary. Washington (DC): National Academies Press (US); 2013 February 6. Retrieved April 24, 2023, from https://www.ncbi.nlm.nlm.nih.gov/books/NBK207262/.

Kunde, L., (2016). Rebuilding lives after loss. How men and women grieve differently.

Grief and Loss Center of North Texas. Retrieved from https://www.bing.com/search?   Pglt=41&q=   Lisa+Kunde+%2c+how+men+and+women+grievedifferently&cvid=38f86da14ac245

Losing a Sibling: A different kind of grief (N. A.). Retrieved from Losing a Sibling: A Different Kind of Grief (sciencecare.com). https://www.sciencecare.com/blog/losing-a-sibling-a-different kinds of grief.

Luggen, A. S., & Meiner, S. E. (2001). NGNA core curriculum for gerontological nursing. St. Louis, MO: Mosby.

Mason, V., Dowling, S. (2016). Bereavement in the Lives of People with Intellectual Disabilities. Intellectual Disability and Health. Psychological intervention for people with learning disabilities who have experienced bereavement: a case study illustration. *British Journal of Learning Disabilities,* 31, pp. 37-41.

Mayo Clinic. Broken heart syndrome. Retrieved April 5, 2023, from https://www.bing.com/search?pglt=43&q=Mayo+Clinic%2C+Broken+heart+syndrome&cvid=7d1b69acf2d74e21b6368ba44870cb1b&aqs=e.

McKeown, J. (2023). Assisted suicide in the United States: Where is it legal? Catholic News Agency.

Oxford English Dictionary. (2003). Oxford University Press. United Kingdom.

Robinson, L., & Segal, J., (2023). Grief & Loss. Coping with Losing a Pet. Retrieved fromhttps://www.helpguide.org/articles/grief/coping-with-losing-a-pet.htm. March 2023.

Shenk, M. (2012). "Paternal Investment and Status-Related Child outcomes: Father's death affects early adolescent's futures in developing world (2012, December 17) retrieved May 5, 2023, from https://phys.org/news/2012-12-father-death-affects-early- adolescents.html. PHYS.ORG. University of Missouri-Columbia.

Sherpa, S. (2021). Gilmore Health News. A patient's guide to medical malpractice: Essential information for every individual. Retrieved from: https://www.gilmorehealth.com/medical-malpractice.

Sloan, M. (2012). Getting Through Grief. Prolonged grief disorder can emerge after someone close has passed away. Here is how to recognize the signs. Harvard Medical School. Harvard's Men's health Watch. Mind and Mood. Harvard Health Publishing.

Sullivan, A. (2021). How to grieve the death of a pet. *Mental Health,* October 2021.

The Holy Bible- King James Version, (KJV) Holman Bible publishers, Nashville, Tennessee.

Tuffrey-Wijne, I. (2011) People with intellectual disabilities. In Death, dying and social differences. 2nd edition. Edited by Oliviere D, Monroe B, Payne

S. Oxford: Oxford University Press Tyson-Rawson, K. (1996). Adolescent response to a death of a parent. In Corr, C. A.

Balik, D. E. (Eds.), *Handbook of adolescent death and bereavement,* Springer Publishing Company. (pp.155-172).

Verrett, B., (2023). What does the Bible Say About Suicide? Bible Study Tools.

Webster, M. (2022) *The Merriam-Webster Dictionary, New Edition. https// www.amazon.com, Mass-Market Paperback.*

Williams, A. (N. D.) The Psychological Effects of Father's Death on Daughters. *Family.* Retrieved from How to change people's bad impression about me (ehow.co.uk).

May 5, 2023, from https:// www.ehow.co.uk/info_8645657_psychological-effects-father's-death-daughters-.html

Wilson, D., Shiffman, J., Morrison, B., & Dwyer, (2015). Helpless and Hooked. A Reuters Investigation. Newborns die after being sent home with mothers struggling to kick drug addictions.

World Council of Churches (1982). "Humanity and Wholeness of Persons with Disabilities." Report on Consultation held at Sao Paulo, 23-30 November 1981. Geneva: WCC.

Printed in the United States
by Baker & Taylor Publisher Services